Grade 5

Addison-Wesley Mathematics

Building Thinking Skills Workbook

Addison-Wesley Publishing Company

*Menlo Park, California ■ Reading, Massachusetts ■ New York
Don Mills, Ontario ■ Wokingham, England ■ Amsterdam ■ Bonn
Sydney ■ Singapore ■ Tokyo ■ Madrid ■ San Juan*

ISBN 0-201-27519-8

3 4 5 6 7 8 9 10 - HC - 95 94 93 92 91

Table of Contents

1-1 Using Math Language 1
1-2 It's In the Cards 2
1-3 Estimating with Compatible Numbers 3
1-4 What was the Question? 4
1-5 Crack the Code 5
1-6 Making Predictions 6
1-7 Creating Problems for Others 7
1-8 Is It or Isn't It? 8

2-1 Hungry Yet? 9
2-2 Changing Statistics 10
2-3 Comparing and Ordering 11
2-4 Rounding for Prizes 12
2-5 Supermarket Stumpers 13
2-6 A Day in the Life 14
2-7 Break the Bank 15
2-8 Decimal Decisions I 16
2-9 Decimal Decisions II 17
2-10 Income Tax Time 18
2-11 Data Matching 19

3-1 Name That Meai 20
3-2 What's the Score? 21
3-3 Read the Receipts 22
3-4 Debug the Problems 23
3-5 Making the Connection 24
3-6 Hitting on the Road 25
3-7 What's the Rule? 26
3-8 The Best Prices in the Universe 27
3-9 Spending Limits 28
3-10 Making Tracks 29
3-11 Using Compensation 30
3-12 Lunch at Major Fowler's 31

4-1 Lunch Specials 32
4-2 Shopping Patterns 33
4-3 Distorted Graph Information 34
4-4 Determining Scales 35
4-5 Scrambled Eggs 36
4-6 Make the Best Guess 37
4-7 Park Funds and Fun 38
4-8 Fact or Opinion 39
4-9 Using a Table 40
4-10 Estimating Sums 41
4-11 Enough or Not Enough? 42

5-1 A Multiplication Shortcut 43
5-2 Ring the Numbers 44
5-3 Another Multiplication Shortcut 45
5-4 Problems Without Numbers 46
5-5 Squares and More Squares 47
5-6 Breaking Apart Numbers 48
5-7 Minutes and Days 49
5-8 Talking on the Phone 50
5-9 What's Cooking at the Video Store? 51
5-10 Foreign Exchange 52
5-11 Using Your Calculator's Memory 53
5-12 Exotic Animal Rentals 54

6-1 Place the Towns 55
6-2 Crack the Code 56
6-3 Using Meters, Centimeters, and Millimeters 57
6-4 Wrapping it Up 58
6-5 Estimating Driving Distances 59
6-6 Estimating Capacity 60
6-7 Metric Olympics 61
6-8 On the Road 62
6-9 Meeting Hands 63
6-10 Making Predictions Using a Table 64

7-1 Quick and Easy 65
7-2 Souvenirs Here! 66
7-3 Pail of Peanuts 67
7-4 Match the Quotients 68
7-5 Catalog Confusion 69
7-6 More That Meets the Eye! 70
7-7 Averages 71
7-8 Blast Off! 72
7-9 What's My Number? 73
7-10 Unit Pricing 74
7-11 Marsha's Mosaics 75
7-12 Ask Abacus 76

8-1 Making Changes 77
8-2 The Happy Camper 78
8-3 Loading Little Leaguers 79
8-4 Find the Answers 80
8-5 Egyptian Division 81
8-6 Creating Problems for Others 82
8-7 Missing Digits 83
8-8 Sports Patterns 84
8-9 Developing Decimal Number Sense 85
8-10 Not Enough Gas 86

9-1 Fractional Figures 87
9-2 Swap Shop 88
9-3 Equivalent Fractions 89
9-4 A New Class 90
9-5 Fractions in the Multiplication Table 91
9-6 Number Patterns 92
9-7 Think Logically 93
9-8 Redeemit's Swap Shop: The Sequel 94
9-9 Geoboard Areas 95
9-10 A Safe Path 96
9-11 Labels with Tables 97

10-1 A Piece of Pizza 98
10-2 In Between 99
10-3 At the Old Seaport 100
10-4 In the Water 101
10-5 Solutions Without Problems 102
10-6 A Slice of the Pie 103
10-7 A Carpentry Project 104
10-8 Addition Clues 105
10-9 Say Cheese 106
10-10 Domino Math 107
10-11 Advanced Domino Math 108

11-1 Concentration 109
11-2 Sir Wexford's Quest 110
11-3 Stranger Than Fiction! 111
11-4 Pattern Possibilities 112
11-5 Fever! 113
11-6 Capacity Confusion 114
11-7 How Heavy Is That Hamster 115
11-8 Treasure Hunt Derby 116

12-1 Playing Fields 117
12-2 Athletic Equipment 118
12-3 The Eating Contest 119
12-4 Fraction Action 120
12-5 A Number Trick 121
12-6 Lionel's Burgers 122
12-7 Carpeting Concerns 123
12-8 Hidden Fractions 124
12-9 Tangram Fractions 125

13-1 What is the Rule? 126
13-2 Possible or Impossible Triangles 127
13-3 Angle Measures 128
13-4 Tangrams 129
13-5 All in the Family 130
13-6 The Envelope, Please 131
13-7 Flip Image 132
13-8 Animal Estimates 133
13-9 Tessellations 134
13-10 Circle Designs 135
13-11 Buried Treasure 136
13-12 Slide Image 137

14-1 Club Count 138
14-2 Super Sale Shopping 139
14-3 It's in the Bag! 140
14-4 Directions...But to Where? 141
14-5 Square Away with Percents 142
14-6 Name That Number 143
14-7 Movie Mania 144
14-8 Percent and Measurement 145
14-9 Getting the Most for Your Money 146
14-10 Amusing Problems 147

15-1 Fair or Unfair? 148
15-2 A Fair Choice? 149
15-3 What Are the Chances? 150
15-4 A Class Experiment 151
15-5 And the Winner Is... 152
15-6 Pizza Party 153
15-7 Taking a Sample 154
15-8 Guess What? 155

16-1 Investigating Perimeter 156
16-2 At the Movies 157
16-3 Lisa's Luncheon Shop 158
16-4 Figure It Out 159
16-5 Making Sails 160
16-6 Try It With Triangles 161
16-7 Areas of Parallelograms 162
16-8 Developing Consumer Skills 163
16-9 Finding Surface Area 164

Name ______________________________

Using Math Language

OFFICIALS PREDICT INCREASED
USE OF MATH LANGUAGE

National officials estimate that within the next decade, the use of math language will continue to rise. These experts say that math is already the "common denominator" when people of different cultures communicate.

You can hear mathematical expressions right in your neighborhood. Go to any grocery store. You might hear people say things like "I'll take two score tomatoes" instead of asking for 40 tomatoes, or "Give me a gross of those peaches" instead of requesting 12 dozen of the fruit.

One official stated proudly, "Ten years ago, only one fourth of the people we spoke to used math language frequently. But in this decade, the number has doubled. Now about fifty percent say they use math language all the time!" Just imagine the progress that will be made in the next half-century.

Reread the article to choose the math words that are unfamiliar or unclear to you. Determine their meanings, either from the context in which they appear in the article or by using a dictionary. Then write each of these words in a sentence that shows you understand its meaning.

Name ______________________________

It's in the Cards

For each number from 1 to 20 formulate a numerical expression that uses the numbers 1, 2, 3, and 4; 1 or more of the 4 operations (+, −, ×, ÷); and parentheses, if necessary. Operations and parentheses maybe used more than once.

Example: $5 = 3 \times (4 \div 2) - 1$

1 = ______________________ 11 = ______________________

2 = ______________________ 12 = ______________________

3 = ______________________ 13 = ______________________

4 = ______________________ 14 = ______________________

5 = ______________________ 15 = ______________________

6 = ______________________ 16 = ______________________

7 = ______________________ 17 = ______________________

8 = ______________________ 18 = ______________________

9 = ______________________ 19 = ______________________

10 = ______________________ 20 = ______________________

Name ______________________________

Estimating with Compatible Numbers

You can use compatible numbers to estimate sums, differences, products, and quotients.

Example:

Mark is furnishing his apartment. He buys 2 lamps for $49 each and 4 rugs for $23 each.

Think: $49 is about $50. ⟶ $2 \times 50 = 100$
$23 is about $25. ⟶ $4 \times 25 = 100$
$100 + 100 = 200$ The lamps and rugs will cost about $200.

Example:

$73 + 26 + 87 \rightarrow \mathbf{75} + \mathbf{25} + 87 = 187$
or
$\mathbf{75} + \mathbf{25} + \mathbf{90} = 190$

Both estimates make sense.

Use compatible numbers and mental math to estimate the answers.

1. $51 \times 3 \times 2$ ______ **2.** $49 + 52 + 47$ ______ **3.** $26 \times 5 \times 4$ ______

4. $76 \div 24$ ______ **5.** $5 \times 19 \times 7$ ______ **6.** $98 \div 4$ ______

7. Rita bought 3 chairs for $47 each and 5 pillows for $18.95 each. About how much did she spend? ______________

8. Albert bought a bookcase for $194 and 3 plants for $24 each. He also bought 24 used books for $2.99 each. About how much did he spend? ______________

9. Wanda bought 5 travel books for $22.95 each, 3 maps for $1.98 each, and a datebook for $4.05. About how much did she spend? ______________

Name ______________________________

What Was the Question?

The table shows items for sale at the gift shop at the national park.

PARK GIFT SHOP					
Map	$4	Trail guide	$ 3	Poster	$ 6
T-shirt	$8	Sweatshirt	$10	Cap	$ 7
Sunglasses	$5	Calendar	$14	Binoculars	$22

Below are answers to questions frequently asked about prices of items in the gift shop. For each answer, make up a question that could go with it.

For example, *Total of $11* could be the answer to the question, *What is the cost for a map and a cap?*

1. Answer: Change is $3 ______________________________

2. Answer: Total is $25 ______________________________

3. Answer: Total is $16 ______________________________

4. Answer: Difference is $4 ______________________________

5. Answer: $15 ______________________________

Name ______________________________

Crack the Code

How old were the oldest players who played in a major professional sport? The oldest basketball player was 42 when he retired. The oldest football player was just a few years older. But the oldest person to play Major League baseball was 59!
To find out who he was, first look at the value for the variable in each row. Then ring the letter in that row next to the expression with the *greatest* value. Write this letter in the space above the number for the row in the code at the bottom. The first one is done for you.

1.	$n = 3$	R. $n + 3$	(E.) $3 \times n$	C. $n - 3$
2.	$y = 4$	T. $y - 2$	Y. $y - 4$	I. $y \times 2$
3.	$r = 2$	T. $r + 3$	S. $r - 2$	L. $r \times 2$
4.	$t = 8$	P. $t - 2$	A. $t \times 2$	O. $t + 2$
5.	$p = 12$	A. $p + 8$	B. $p - 3$	E. $3 \times p$
6.	$n = 10$	H. $n + 15$	R. $n \times 2$	C. $n - 5$
7.	$s = 6$	B. $2 \times s$	A. $s + 7$	K. $s - 5$
8.	$z = 15$	H. $z + 15$	L. $z + 20$	E. $2 \times z$
9.	$y = 5$	W. $3 \times y$	T. $y + 15$	P. $y \times 5$
10.	$t = 20$	C. $t + 10$	R. $t - 10$	O. $t \times 1$
11.	$r = 9$	A. $r + 6$	S. $36 - r$	J. $r \times 2$
12.	$m = 7$	Y. $m + m$	S. $m - m$	G. $m \times m$

					E						
11	4	3	10	6	1	8	9	7	2	12	5

Name ______________________________

Making Predictions

You can use line graphs to make predictions. The graphs below show the sales of the movie *Math Monsters from Mars* in two different video stores. The sales are for its first 6 weeks in the store. Study the pattern in each graph to predict the sales for the movie in weeks 7, 8, 9, and 10.

1. Movie Sales at Laser Videos

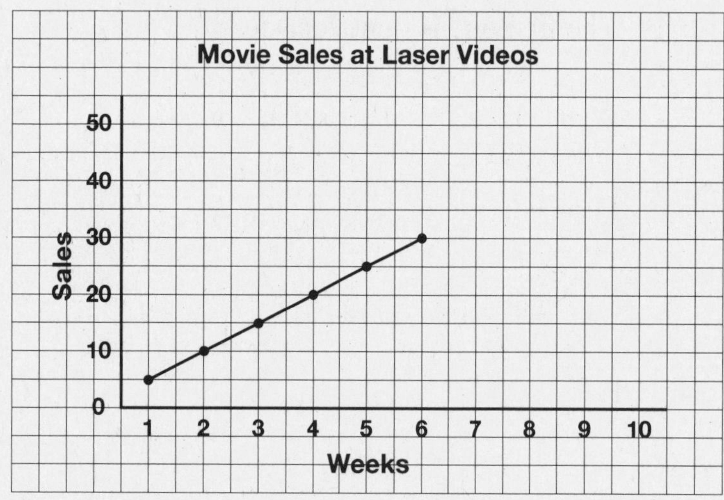

____

2. Movie Sales at Space Videos

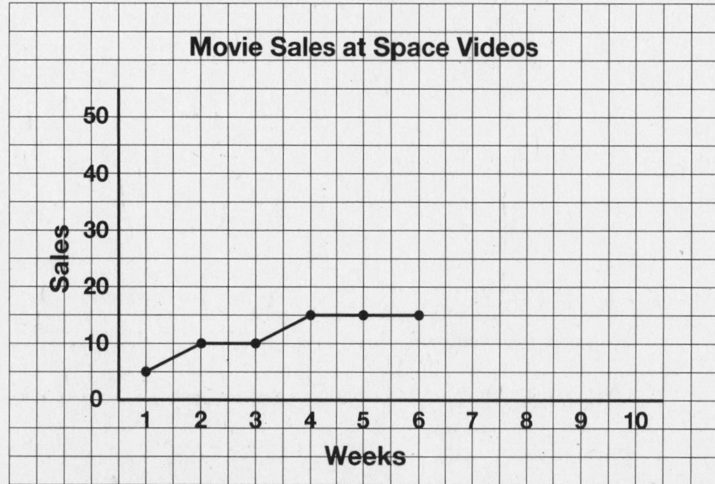

____

Name ______________________________

Creating Problems for Others

> Dear Family,
> Your child has been learning how to solve one-step problems. The two of you can create some problems for others.

Use the price list below. Make up four problems that can be solved using one operation, and one problem whose solution requires two operations. Find the solution to your own problems before giving them to others.

YVETTE AND GUY'S PET SUPPLIES	
Item	Y and G's low price
Doggie Delights—1 bag lasts a week	$6 a bag
Fancy Fish Food	$4 a container
Kitten Yummies—2 cans last a week	$2 a can
Turtle Gymnasium—*includes mats*	$12; 2 for $20
Gerbil Songbooks—*NEW!*	$3 each with guitar, $28
Poodle Polish—was $3, new low price	6 bottles for $12

1. ______________________________

2. ______________________________

3. ______________________________

4. ______________________________

5. ______________________________

Name ______________________________

Is It or Isn't It?

Sometimes it is easy to tell if a number is an estimate:

". . . 200,000 people watched the parade."

Sometimes it is not so easy:

". . . 50,500 in the stadium today."

Were there *exactly* 50,500 people in the stadium, or *about* 50,500 people? What do you think?

Look at the newspaper headlines below. Decide whether each is an estimate or an exact amount. Explain your answer.

1. 9 MILLION SOLD
2. 1,000 HIRED AT PLANT
3. JETS WIN BY 50
4. WADE SIGNS $2,500,000 CONTRACT
5. BOOK SELLS 500,000 COPIES

1. ______________________________

____

2. ______________________________

____

3. ______________________________

____

4. ______________________________

____

5. ______________________________

____

Name ______________________________

Hungry Yet?

Read each world record below. Write the missing digit. Then place the letter over the digit at the bottom of the page to answer the riddle.

1. Greatest number of people at a barbecue: thirty-five thousand, seventy two: 35,__72. (W)

2. Heaviest chocolate egg: seven thousand, five hundred sixty-one pounds: 7,__61. (N)

3. Largest hamburger: five thousand, six pounds: 5,00__ (E)

4. Heaviest pancake: four thousand, two hundred thirty-eight pounds: 4,__38 (A)

5. Largest cherry pie: twenty-five thousand, eight hundred ninety pounds: 25,8__0 (F)

6. Heaviest salad: one hundred fourteen thousand, eight hundred eighty-five pounds: 11__,885 (U)

7. Largest sundae: thirty-three thousand, six hundred sixteen pounds: __3,616 (L)

8. Largest portion of mashed potatoes: eighteen thousand, two hundred sixty pounds: 1__,260 (G)

9. Largest sausage: five thousand, nine hundred seventeen feet: 5,9__7 (O)

What does a chicken speak?

__	__	__	__		__	__	__	__	__	__	__	__
9	1	0	3		3	2	5	8	4	2	8	6

Name ______________________________

Changing Statistics

Read each statement. Then answer the question using mental math and place value.

1. The largest country in the world is the Soviet Union, with an area of about 8,647,000 square miles. If the Soviet Union lost 30,000 square miles, what would its area be?

____

2. A recent population estimate for the world was 5,128,000,000. What was the population when it had grown by 2,000,000?

____

3. One of Jupiter's moons, called Hera, is 7,292,940 miles from Jupiter. If it were pulled 200,000 miles closer by Jupiter's gravity, how far from the planet would it be?

____

4. In the years 1820 to 1930, a total of 37,762,012 people immigrated to the United States. If an additional 3,000,000 had immigrated, how many people would have arrived here?

____

5. In a recent census, the population of Houston, Texas, was 1,611,382. If an additional 7,000 people had been counted, what would have been the population?

____

6. Recently, it was estimated that there are 139,041,000 automobiles in the United States. If 30,000,000 were suddenly taken off the roads, how many would be left?

____

7. About 184,700,000 Americans live in or around cities. If an additional six million people moved to the cities, what would the total be?

____

Name ____________________

Comparing and Ordering

Dear Family,
We are studying, comparing, and ordering whole numbers in class. This game reinforces needed skills. After each round you might wish to discuss successful strategies.

Number of Players: 2 or more

Materials Needed: number cube, or spinner numbered 1-6, index card

How to Play: Each line shown below is used for a different game.

1. ___ ___ , ___ ___ ___ > ___ ___ , ___ ___ ___

2. ___ ___ , ___ ___ ___ < ___ ___ , ___ ___ ___

3. ___ ___ , ___ ___ ___ > ___ ___ , ___ ___ ___

> ___ ___ , ___ ___ ___

4. ___ ___ , ___ ___ ___ < ___ ___ , ___ ___ ___ < 47,562

5. ___ ___ , ___ ___ ___ > ___ ___ , ___ ___ ___ > 28,031

Each player copies line 1 on an index card. Take turns rolling the cube or spinning the spinner. With each toss, all players write the number shown in any blank space on their card. Once a number is written in a space, it may not be moved. Game 1 will require 10 tosses or spins. In each game the object is to make a true number sentence. If only one player succeeds, he or she is the winner. If more than one player makes a true sentence, each subtracts her or his smaller number from her or his greater number. The player with the greatest difference is then the winner.

Each game may consist of several rounds if you wish.

Name ______________________________

Rounding for Prizes

Welcome to Round You Go, in which you compete against an opponent for wonderful prizes.

The rules are simple. We will show you a prize from our galaxy of gifts. To score a point, just make a better estimate of its value rounded to the place we tell you. Your opponent always goes first so you can also score a point by recognizing that your opponent has made the best possible estimate.

For example, the first prize you will be bidding for is a new TV!

Value of TV: $459 Round to the nearest $100.

Your opponent says $400. Can you make a better estimate?

____

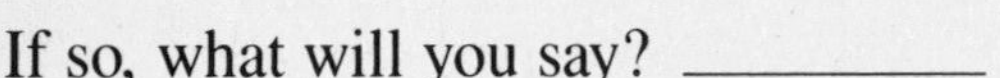

If so, what will you say? __________

Try your hand at these lovely items. Good luck!

Item	Value	Rounded to nearest:	Opponent says:	You say:
Gold necklace!	$ 185	ten	$ 180	
Living room set!	$ 2,440	thousand	$ 2,000	
Camcorder!	$ 1,259	hundred	$ 1,200	
A European vacation!	$ 3,509	thousand	$ 3,000	
A racing bike!	$ 274	ten	$ 270	
A diamond ring!	$ 9,509	hundred	$ 9,600	
A new car	$14,605	thousand	$14,000	

Name ____

Supermarket Stumpers

Solve each problem. You may want to draw a picture.

1. At Dean's Supermarket, the fruits and vegetables are in one aisle, canned food in another, frozen food in another, and baked goods in another. Fruits and vegetables are on one end. Baked goods are between canned and frozen food. Canned food is not in an end aisle. Which aisles are on either side of canned foods?

____

____

2. Grapefruit, grapes, lemons, limes, and oranges are all on one side of the fruit and vegetable aisle. Grapefruit are between limes and lemons. Lemons are between grapefruit and grapes. Limes are between oranges and grapefruit. As you walk down the aisle, you come to oranges first. What will be the last fruit you come to?

____

____

3. The macaroni is all on one side of an aisle on two shelves. The bottom shelf is filled with 13 feet of spaghetti and 7 feet of linguini. The top shelf has 8 feet of rigatoni with the rest of the shelf filled by different kinds of macaroni. How many feet of shelving are left over for these different kinds?

____

4. Milk, butter, yogurt, and orange juice are in a row in the refrigerated case. The milk and orange juice are 32 ft apart. The distance from the milk to the butter is 9 ft. The yogurt and orange juice are 7 ft apart. How far must you walk from the butter to the yogurt?

____

Name ______________________________

A Day in the Life

Read the story. Inside each set of parentheses are choices. Circle the one that makes the most sense according to the information in the story.

Marie, who likes to talk in riddles, was telling her math class about herself and her weekend. She began by describing herself. "Let's just say that I am x years old. My (younger, older) brother Daniel, who is $x + 3$ years old, and I spent the weekend with our (grandmother, cousin) Carmen, who likes doing the same things as we do although she is $x + 12$ years old. Anyway, on Saturday, the three of us took a bus to a carnival. Carmen had to pay y dollars for the bus ride. The driver charged Daniel and me only (y + \$1, y − \$1) because we're younger. We've made this same trip in the past. It usually takes 25 minutes. Today being Saturday, there was very little traffic. The whole trip took only ($25 - n$, $n + 25$) minutes. Once again, when we went to pay admission, Daniel and I were lucky. It cost each of us a dollars to get in. It cost Carmen (a + \$2, a − \$1). Once inside, there was no extra charge for the rides, but the lines were really long. We estimated that the line for the haunted castle was m minutes. But the line for the Rumbling Thunder roller coaster was much longer. We estimated it at ($3 \times m$, $m + 2$) minutes. No ride is *that* good! Well, we did wait and when we finally got to the front, we found out that you had to be at least h inches tall to be allowed on the ride. When they measured us, they found that I was $h - 2$ inches, Daniel was $h + 4$ inches, and Carmen was exactly h inches tall. Only (1, 2, 3) of us got to test Rumbling Thunder. I don't have to tell you who was unhappy, do I?

Name ____________________

Break the Bank

Dear Family,
We are studying decimal place value in class. This game will help reinforce the idea that in the decimal system each place has a value ten times the value of the place to its right.

Number of Players: 2 or 3

Materials Needed: two number cubes; a supply of pennies, dimes, dollar bills, and a $10 bill (either real or play money); a game board for each player as below

$10.00	$1.00	$0.10	$0.01

How to Play:

The object of the game is to get the $10 bill.

Select a banker for each game. That person distributes the money and also plays.

Take turns. Roll the number cubes and multiply the numbers shown. Take a number of pennies equal to the product.

Whenever a player accumulates ten pennies, they must be exchanged for one dime, ten dimes for one dollar, and ten dollar bills for the winning $10 bill. It is the player's responsibility to trade when appropriate. If an error is made and another player points it out, the erring player loses his or her next turn.

Name ______________________________

Decimal Decisions I

Read and follow each set of directions.

1. Place a decimal point in each set of digits to form a number that is between the given numbers.

A 4107

A number between 4 and 5 ________

A number between 40 and 50 ________

A number between 400 and 500 ________

B 3052

A number between 2 and 4 ________

A number between 30 and 40 ________

A number between 300 and 400 ________

C 9480

A number between 9 and 90 ________

A number between 90 and 900 ________

A number between 900 and 9,000 ________

2. Use 6019, make up your own examples and complete them.

A number between ______ and ______ ______

A number between ______ and ______ ______

A number between ______ and ______ ______

3. Start with 6.037 and write the number that fits each description.

A number that is one tenth greater ________

A number that is three hundredths less ________

A number that is two thousandths greater ________

Name ______________________________

Decimal Decisions II

Copy and cut out these 20 numeral cards. Then use all of the cutouts to make true number sentences by placing them in the frames. Use each card only once.

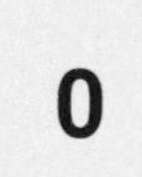 0	0	0	0	0	0	0	0	2	 2
3	 4	4	5	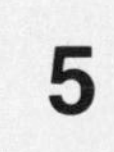 5	7	7	8	8	9

1. $3.56 < \square . \square\,\square < 3.58$

2. $28.9 > \square\,\square . \square > 28.7$

3. $21.44 + \square . \square = 21.94$

4. $6.08 - \square . \square\,\square = 6.01$

5. $2.77 + \square . \square\,\square = 2.79$

6. $4.89 < \square . \square\,\square < 4.91$

7. $0.41 > \square . \square\,\square > 0.39$

Name ______________________________

Income Tax Time

The Internal Revenue Service suggests that when you fill out your income tax forms you round each amount to the nearest whole dollar. Follow their advice in answering the questions below. In each case, round the numbers before you calculate.

If an amount on one line of the form should be $104.62, they allow you to write $105.00. If another line should be $83.39, you may write $83.00.

1. If you had three jobs and earned incomes of $15,805.51, $9,311.12, and $6,849.90, what would you write on the line of the form that asks for total wages earned?

____

2. If you earned the following amounts of interest on bank accounts, what would you write on the line that asks for total interest earned: $91.49, $23.85, $181.09, $50.50?

____

3. In some cases, contributions to charity help reduce the amount you owe in taxes. If you contributed $55.55, $25.00, and $39.75 to charities, what would you write on the line that asks for total contributions?

____

4. Workers who earn tips must declare those amounts as income. If a waiter kept this record for a year, what would he declare as income from tips?

____

Month	Income	Month	Income
Jan	$410.50	Jul	$269.59
Feb	$585.15	Aug	$304.71
Mar	$508.09	Sep	$585.15
Apr	$530.50	Oct	$410.50
May	$545.10	Nov	$585.15
Jun	$680.95	Dec	$735.45

Name ______________________________

Data Matching

Match each set of data in the box with the problem in which it makes the most sense. Then solve the problem.

1. Charles spent ________ , ________ and ________ on lunch items in the school cafeteria. He paid with a $5 bill. How much change did he receive? ________

2. The temperature on five days last week was ________ F, ________ F, ________ F, ________ F, and ________ F. What was the difference between the high and low temperatures? ________

3. All ________ students in the fifth grade are going on a bus trip. If each bus can carry ________ students, will ________ buses be enough? ________

4. Margaret lives ________ blocks from school. It takes her ________ minutes to walk each way. If Carry lives ________ blocks from school, how long do you estimate it takes her to walk to school? ____________

5. Vincent earned ________ , ________ , and ________ during three weeks of mowing lawns. He is trying to save ________ . How much more does he need? ________

6. The school day is ________ hours long, and each period lasts for ________ minutes. If period ________ is about to start, how many periods are left in the school day? ________

8 15 16	68°F 74°F 76°F 63°F 79°F	\$0.95 \$0.49 \$0.55
\$8.50 \$7.75 \$9.00 \$30.00	6 45 6	153 30 5

Name ________________________________

Name That Meal

After the game, five of the Pirates dropped anchor at Captain Jack's Seafood Restaurant. Use the menu at Captain Jack's to solve the problems below.

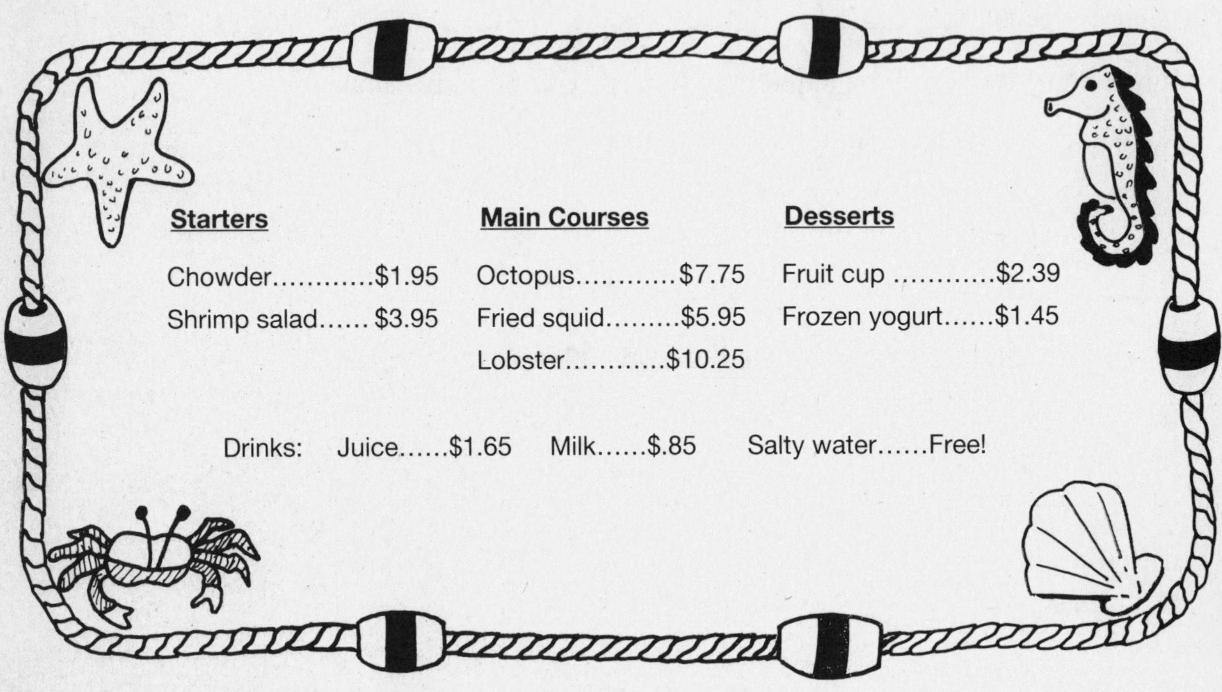

1. Rodney ordered the chowder, a main course, and milk. He spent about $9. What main course did he order?

____

2. Tomas ordered a starter, octopus, fruit cup, and a drink. He spent about $14. What did he start with, and what did he drink?

____

3. Winona spent about $2 less than Tomas. She ordered shrimp salad, a main course, and juice. Which main course did she order?

____

4. Eddie spent about $13 on his meal. He had a starter, a main course, a dessert, and a drink. What might he have ordered?

____

Name ___

What's the Score?

1. Scoring in the New World Basketball League is as follows:

1 point for a free throw
2 points for a field goal
3 points for a longer field goal
4 points for a field goal with closed eyes

Use the clues to complete the scoreboard.

Quarter	1	2	3	4	Final Score
Bunnies					
Poodles					

At the end of the first quarter, the score was 37–32 in favor of the Poodles.

In the second quarter, the Poodles scored 8 field goals, two 3-point field goals, one 4-point field goal, and 3 free throws to increase their lead to 6 points.

At the end of the third quarter, the Poodles saw their lead slip to only 2 points. The Bunnies scored 32 points in that quarter.

In the fourth quarter, the Bunnies scored 5 field goals, four 3-point field goals, 3 with their eyes closed, and 6 free throws. They won by 2 points. What was the final score?

___

2. Make up a scoreboard problem like the one you just solved. Make up the names of the teams and use the same scoring system. Solve your problem first, then give it to classmates to solve.

Name ______________________________

Read the Receipts

Use front-end digits and adjust to estimate the total for each receipt.
Use your estimate to answer the question that follows.

1.

Store 013 4/11/90

THANK YOU

$4.77
$3.24
$8.55
$9.75
$3.45

You have $31.

Do you have enough money? __________

2.

Store 103 5/03/90

THANK YOU

$3.95
$6.08
$7.15
$3.42
$9.79

You have $30.

Do you have enough money? __________

3.

Store 132 7/23/89

THANK YOU

$9.43
$4.66
$5.79
$9.99
$3.05
$2.95

You have $30.
About how much more will you need?

____

4.

Store 045 6/1/90

THANK YOU

$1.89
$8.45
$5.13
$6.59
$4.88
$7.55

You have $40.
Can you also buy a $4 box of laundry soap?

____

Solve.

5. You bought items with the following prices: $6.95, $3.35, $7.15, $8.59, and $12.95, and returned bottles worth $3. If you pay with two $20 bills, about how much change will you get?

____

Name ______________________________

Debug the Problems

Solve using the Guess and Check strategy.

1. A fish ate 39 bugs in 3 days. Each day it ate 5 more bugs than on the previous day. How many bugs did the fish eat each day?

____

2. A frog ate 96 bugs in 4 days. Each day it ate 10 more bugs than it did on the day before. How many bugs did it eat each day?

____

3. A bird ate 125 bugs in 5 days. Each day it ate 10 more bugs than it did on the previous day. How many bugs did the bird eat each day?

____

4. A bigger bird ate a total of 250 big bugs in 5 days. Each day it ate 15 more than on the day before. How many bugs did it eat each day?

____

5. A Venus's-flytrap swallowed 198 bugs in 6 days. Each day it swallowed 12 more than on the day before. How many bugs did it swallow each day?

____

6. A big bug bothered a little bug for its entire life: 5 days. Each day the bigger bug bothered the littler bug 7 more times than on the day before. How many times did the bigger bug bother the littler bug each day if it bothered it 120 times in all?

____

Name ______________________________

Making the Connection

Look at the pictures of the place value blocks. There are 3 units blocks, 5 tenths blocks, and 4 hundredths blocks.

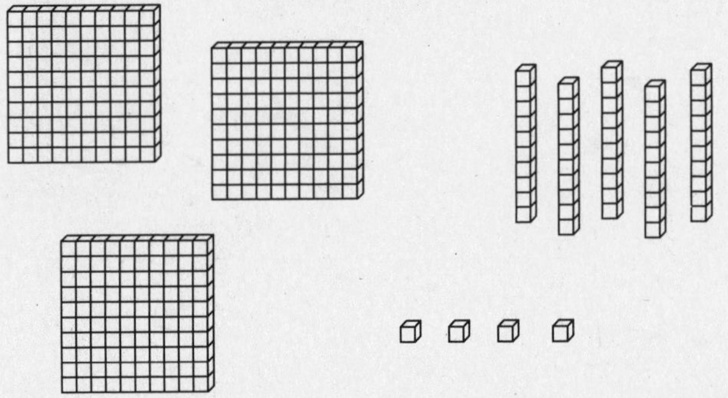

Complete each sentence. Use place value blocks to help you.

1. A units block is made up of _____ tenths blocks, or _____ hundredths blocks.

2. The whole set of blocks pictured is made up of _____ hundredths blocks.

3. The whole set of blocks is made up of _____ tenths blocks with a remainder of _____ hundredths blocks. You can write this as the decimal _____ tenths blocks.

4. You can also express the whole set of blocks as the decimal _____ units blocks.

5. _____ tenths blocks need to be added to the set of blocks to get the number 5.

6. _____ units blocks need to be added to the set of blocks to get the number 7.

Name ______________________________

Hitting on the Road

The map below shows where the teams in the Garden Baseball League are located. Currently, the Pumpkin Seeds, Celery Stalks, and Bean Sprouts are playing their opponents away from home. When they travel, the teams always take the shortest route.

Here is the schedule.
The Seeds are playing the Rhubarb Pies and then the Artichoke Hearts before returning to Pumpkin.
The Stalks are playing in Cucumber and then in Tomato before returning home.
The Sprouts are playing the Artichokes and then have a game in Rhubarb before going back to Bean.

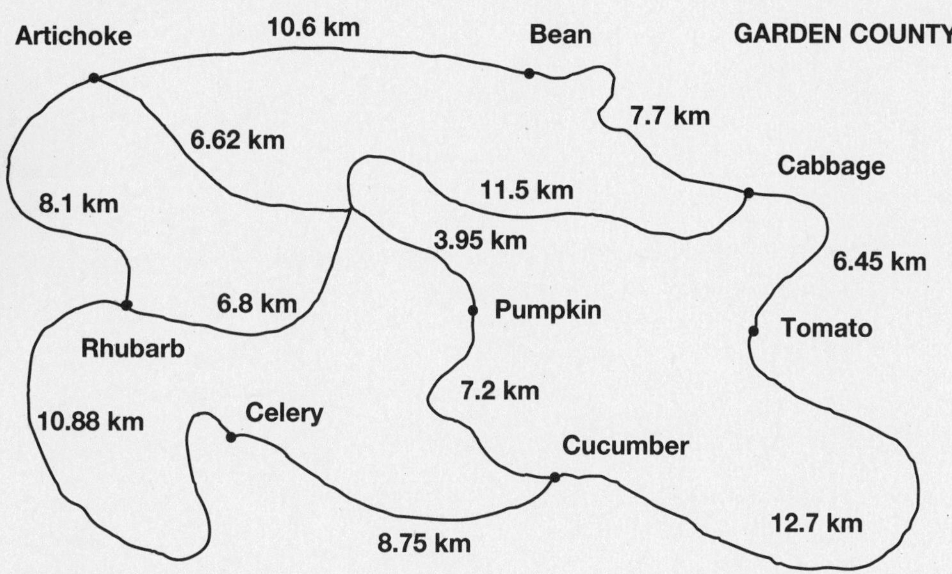

1. Which team traveled the farthest on its trip? ____________

2. Which team drove the shortest distance? ____________

3. Which team would travel farthest if the Sprouts played the Cabbage Leaves instead of the Artichoke Hearts? ____________

4. A Cabbage Leaf scout went to watch the games in Rhubarb, Artichoke, and Tomato. What is the distance of the shortest round-trip route she could have traveled to see the games in that order? ____________

Name ________________________________

What Is the Rule?

Complete each function table. Then complete the function rule.

1.

☆	⊡
3	8
4	10
1	4
5	____
2	6
____	16

The rule is:

2 × ☆ + ____ = ⊡

2.

☆	⊡
1	2
3	____
5	14
4	11
2	____
____	23

The rule is:

3 × ☆ − ____ = ⊡

3.

☆	⊡
2	9
4	15
5	____
3	12
____	6
6	____

The rule is:

____ × ☆ + ____ = ⊡

4.

☆	⊡
1	4
3	14
5	____
____	9
8	39
____	49

The rule is:

____ × ☆ − ____ = ⊡

5.

☆	⊡
1	2
2	6
____	14
____	30
7	26
12	____

The rule is:

____ × ☆ − ____ = ⊡

6.

☆	⊡
1	3.5
3	7.5
5	11.5
4	____
____	5.5
8	____

The rule is:

____ × ☆ + ____ = ⊡

Name ____________________

The Best Prices in the Universe

Shoppers are flocking to Jupiter to take advantage of the low, low prices. Solve each problem. Choose the calculation method that seems best for you.

1. A TV and a VCR together cost $30. The TV costs $20 more than the VCR. What is the price of each?

____

2. A spaceship and a landing craft together sell for $110. The spaceship sells for $100 more than the landing craft. What is the price of each?

____

3. Mike and his two sisters ate at a restaurant famous throughout the galaxy for its low prices. Each had a Saturn salad for $0.75 and Martian meatloaf for $1.50. His sisters had Pluto pastries for $0.60 each, while Mike had a $0.50 space juice. What was the bill for this interplanetary feast?

____

4. Lawrence sells homemade Moon muffins. During one 4-day period, he had total sales of $9. If on each of those days his sales were $0.50 higher than on the previous day, what was the amount of his sales on the first day?

____

Name ______________________________

Spending Limits

Solve each problem. Use blocks to show that your answer is correct.

1. Isabel brought $5 with her to the store to buy fruit. Her mother told her to come back with more than $2 in change. What is the most Isabel can spend?

____

2. Ralph's father gave him $10 to spend at the street fair. His father told him to enjoy himself and make sure he comes back with less than $5 in his pocket. Ralph does not like to spend money. What is the least he can spend at the fair and still follow his father's instructions?

____

3. John had $8.25 with him when he went to the mall. What is the most he could have spent there if he returned home with more than $4.00?

____

4. Krista brought $6.05 to the mall. What is the least she could have spent there if she left with less than $1 in her pocket?

____

5. David's mother gave him $5.50 to spend, and his father gave him $7.50. When he finished spending, he had more than $4.50 left. What is the most he could have spent?

____

Name ______________________

Making Tracks

Solve each problem.

Drawing a diagram may help.

1. A train is going from Apricot to Cauliflower, stopping at Blackberry along the way. It is 18.5 km from Apricot to Cauliflower and 11.8 km from Cauliflower to Blackberry. What is the distance between Apricot and Blackberry? ______________

2. A train starts at Dandelion and makes stops at Earthworm and Freshwater on its journey to Greenville. The route is 25 km long. If it is 6.2 km from Dandelion to Earthworm, and 8.3 km from Freshwater to Greenville, how far is it from Earthworm to Freshwater? ______________

3. The Blossom Special goes from Honeysuckle to Juniper, passing through Ivy. If it is 18.35 km from Honeysuckle to Ivy, and 15.9 km from Ivy to Juniper, how far is the round trip from Honeysuckle to Juniper and back? ______________

4. The train stops at Kiwi, Lemon, and Mango before reaching Orange. Kiwi is 16.56 km west of Mango. Mango is 6.7 km east of Lemon. Lemon is 12.4 km west of Orange. How far is Kiwi from Orange? ______________

Name ____________________

Using Compensation

Complete each statement.

1. Adding 99 is like adding 100 and then subtracting ______.

2. Adding 198 is like adding ____________ and then subtracting ____________.

3. Subtracting 99 is like subtracting 100 and then adding ____.

4. Subtracting 299 is like subtracting ____________ and then adding ____________.

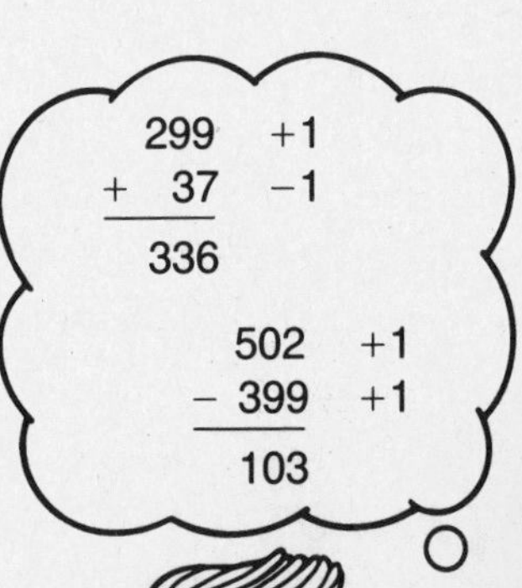

5. Subtracting 404 is like subtracting ____________ and then ____________ 4.

6. Adding 297 is like adding ____________ and then ____________ 3.

7. Adding 1.9 is like adding 2 and then subtracting ________.

8. Adding 3.8 is like adding 4 and then subtracting ________.

9. Subtracting 0.8 is like subtracting ____________ and then adding ____________.

10. Subtracting 9.9 is like subtracting ________________ and ____________ 0.1.

11. Adding ____________ is like adding 10 and ____________ 0.2.

Solve. Use mental math. Explain your method.

12. Frank went shopping. He purchased items for \$12.95, \$20.05, and \$10.95. How much did he spend?

____

Name ______________________________

Lunch at Major Fowler's

Dear Family,
Your child has been learning to use a calculator to solve problems. Work together, with calculators, to find out what each person had for lunch at Major Fowler's Farm Fresh Restaurant.

Lunch at Major Fowler's

Chicken sandwich	$2.95	Corn soup	$1.95	Juice	$0.75
Chicken salad	$3.45	Duck soup	$2.75	Milk	$0.60
Turkey club	$4.95	Cole slaw	$1.45	Tea	$0.45

1. Dana ordered ______________ and ______________. She spent $3.55.

2. Elia ordered ______________, ______________, and ______________. He spent $6.00.

3. Mary ordered ______________, ______________, and 2 ______________. She spent $5.30.

4. Rudy ordered ______________ and 2 ______________. He spent $11.10.

5. Lani was thirsty. She ordered ______________, ______________, and 3 ______________. She paid with a $20 bill and got $10.05 in change.

6. Make up a problem. Find the answer. Give it to a family member to solve.

____

____

____

____

Name ______________________________

Lunch Specials

Following a school lunch of liver and spinach, two friends, Roger and Ralph, decided to survey the students. The question they asked was, "Did you finish your meal?" Much to their surprise, some students did. They reported their findings in the graphs below. Roger used a bar graph; Ralph used a pictograph.

Study the graphs. Then decide whether there is enough information to answer each question. If it is possible, answer the question. If it is not possible, write "not enough information."

Number of Students Who Finished the School Lunch

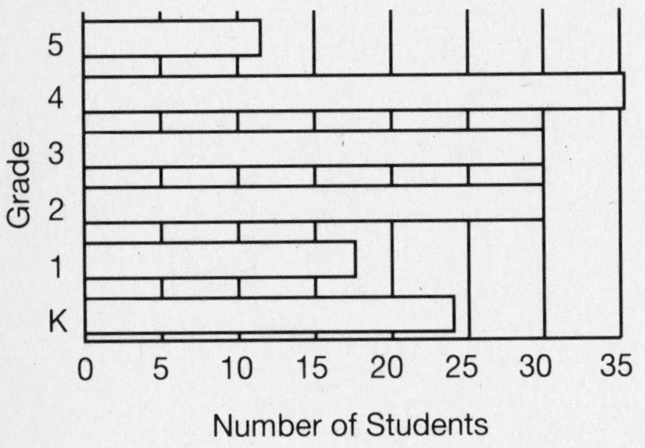

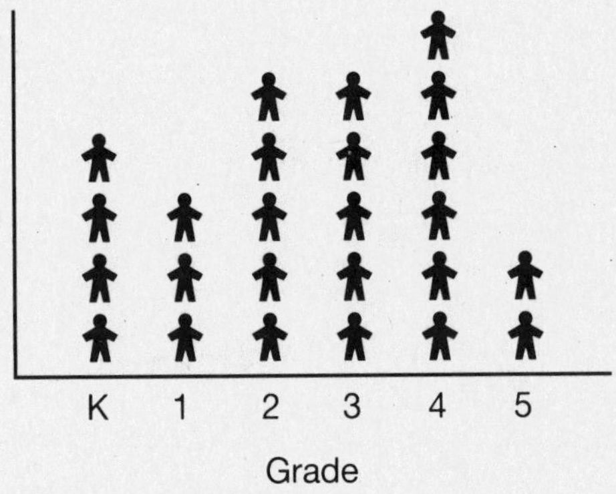

1. How many students were able to finish their liver and spinach?

____

2. How many students did Roger and Ralph ask altogether?

____

3. Grades K, 1, and 2 eat lunch first. Then grades 3, 4, and 5 eat. During which lunch period did more students finish their meal?

____

4. In making his pictograph, Ralph forgot to include a key. You can determine Ralph's key by looking at Roger's graph. How many students does each figure represent in the pictograph?

____

Name ____________________

Shopping Patterns

During the year, many shopping patterns change. For example, less ice cream is sold in January than in July.

The graphs below show shopping patterns you might expect for different purchases. Match each pattern with the most likely item from the list below. Then extend the graph for three months to show how the trend might continue.

1.

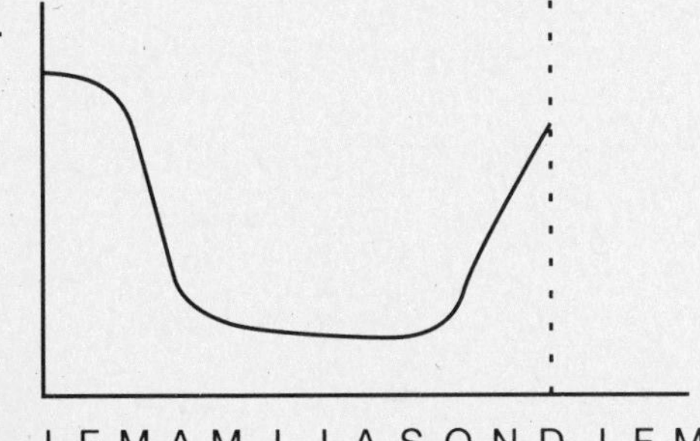

2.

3.

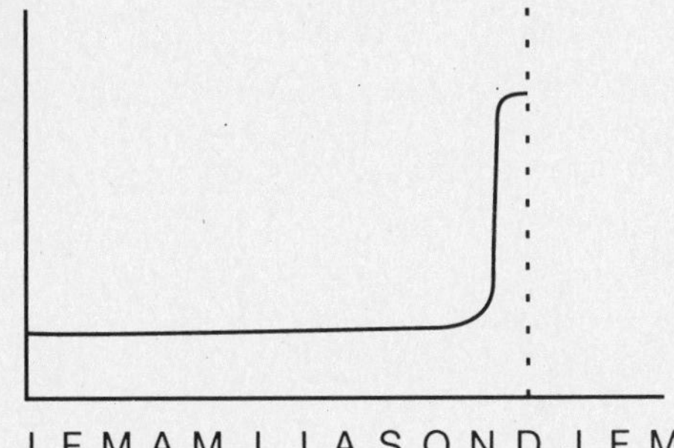

4.

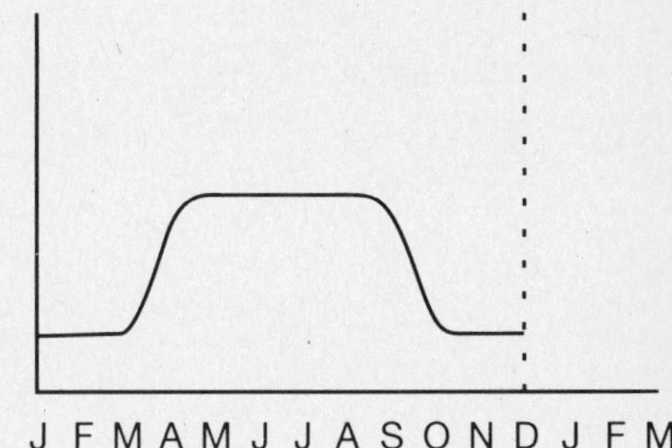

5

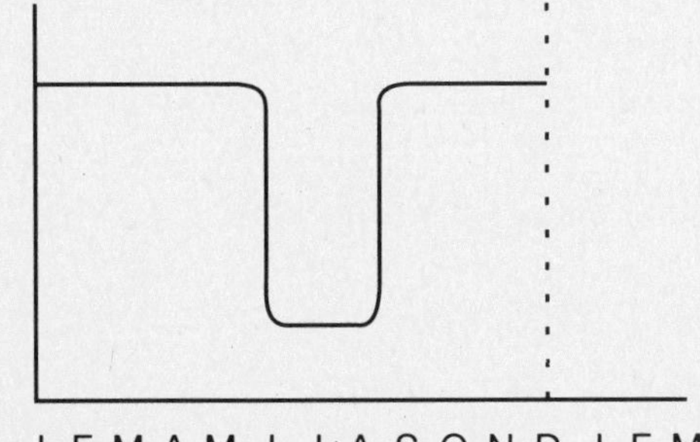

6

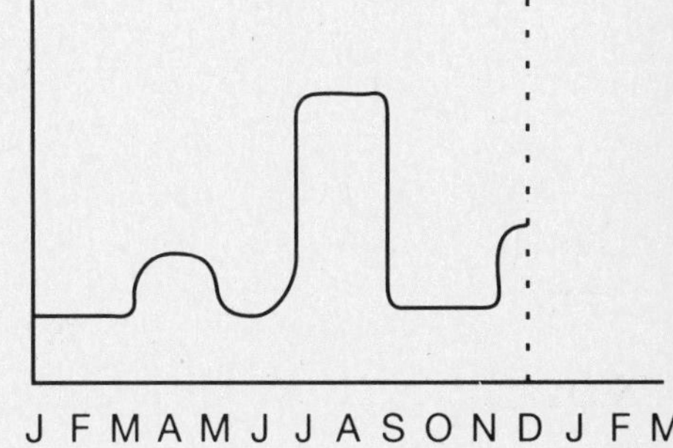

New Year's Eve decorations ____ family travel ____ groceries ____

ski equipment ____ school lunch money ____ baseball cards ____

Name ____________________

Distorted Graph Information

The members of class 5-203 collected money all year to help the school fund. They kept a line graph showing the total amount they had collected by the end of each month. Here is the graph they drew:

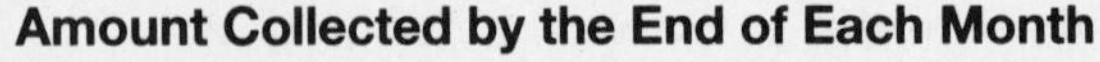

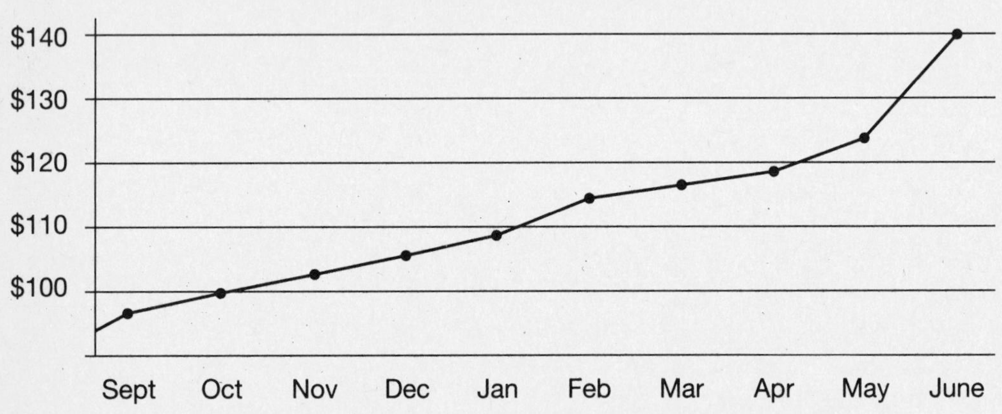

1. When you first examine the graph, how many times greater does the amount at the end of June seem than the amount at the end of September?

____

2. When you look more carefully, you see that this graph has been drawn in a misleading way. What is there about this graph that might cause you to read it incorrectly?

____

____

3. About how much had the class collected by the end of September?

____

4. In which month did they collect the most? ____________

Name ______________________________

Determining Scales

When you make a bar graph you must decide on a reasonable scale to use for your data.

Examine the sets of data below. Each set is the result of a survey of a group of students. For each set, choose the best scale to use for constructing a bar graph of the data. Write the letter of the scale next to the title.

Favorite School Activity _____

- ▶ free play 40
- ▶ rest period 38
- ▶ dreaming 37

Favorite Foods _____

- ▶ turtle soup 7
- ▶ squid 17
- ▶ anchovy ice cream 21

Favorite Pets _____

- ▶ iguana 9
- ▶ snake 8
- ▶ mole 4

Favorite Holiday _____

- ▶ National Hat Week 2
- ▶ National Vegetable Day 1
- ▶ National Children's Day 19

Favorite Teacher _____

- ▶ Mr. Ross N. Bag (baseball coach) 51
- ▶ Mr. Dan D. Lyon (biology) 70
- ▶ Mr. Al Gebra (math) 62

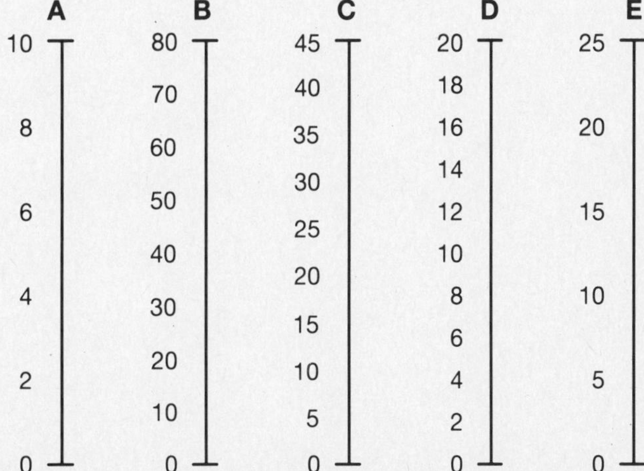

Use with text pages 96-97.

Name ______________________________

Scrambled Eggs

Farmer Jake "Hardboiled" Robinson raises chickens for their eggs. He is a successful farmer, but his record keeping could be a lot better.

During one month, Jake kept records using a bar, line, and pictograph with these titles:

Bar graph: Eggs Gathered Per Week
Line graph: Total Eggs Gathered by End of Each Week
Pictograph: Eggs Gathered Per Day During Week 1

During a flap in the henhouse, everything except the titles got mixed up!

Can you unscramble the titles of the axes, the scales, and the information in the graphs? Help Jake by redrawing them on graph paper so that everything matches. When you finish, you should be able to answer the questions below.

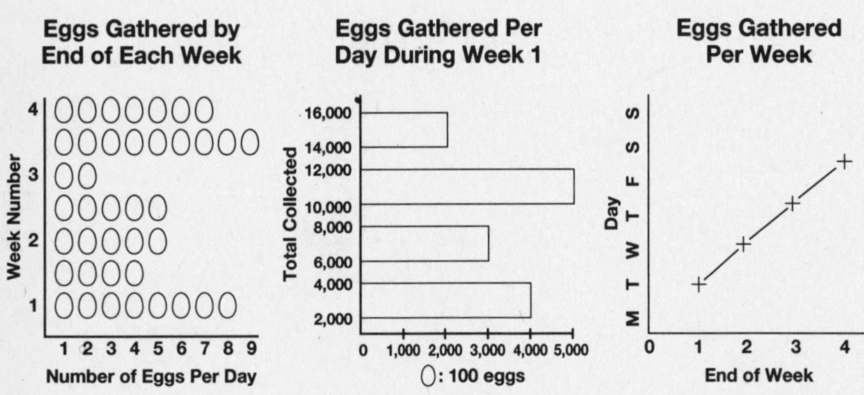

1. During which week did Jake collect the most eggs?

____

2. On which two days of the first week did Jake collect the same number of eggs? ______________________________

3. How many eggs had Jake collected by the end of the third week? ______________________________

Name ___

Make the Best Guess

How good are your estimating skills? Here is a chance to test them against an opponent.

You will need: an opponent, a calculator.

How to Play:
The game consists of 11 rounds. During each round you and your opponent each write numbers from the box you estimate will reach the goal for the round. Three seconds and no pencils allowed! Then verify your estimates with the calculator. The player coming closest to the goal of the round scores 1 point. No points are scored for a tie. After 11 rounds, the player with the highest score is the winner.

75	47	21	29
19	35	25	53
64	77	22	20
30	12	89	36

Round	Goal	Jan	Dan
1	3 numbers whose sum is 100	35 + 36 + 30	64 + 22 + 21
		101	107
			1 point for Jan
2	3 numbers whose sum is 150		
3	2 numbers whose difference is 60		
4	3 numbers whose sum is 200		
5	2 numbers whose product is 750		
6	2 numbers whose quotient is 4		
7	4 numbers whose sum is 100		
8	2 numbers whose difference is 40		
9	5 numbers whose sum is 250		
10	2 numbers whose product is 1,000		
11	2 numbers whose quotient is 3		

Name ______________________________

Park Funds and Fun

To help raise money for the local park, Joseph asked his family for donations to the park fund instead of giving him birthday presents.

He received these contributions:

Sister	$10
Brother	$10
Aunt	$15
Parents	$20
Grandparents	$45

1. What was the mean (average) amount of the gifts Joseph received? ______________________________

2. What was the median? ______________________________

3. What was the mode? ______________________________

4. What was the range? ______________________________

Later that week Joseph's grandparents sold a piece of property. They asked him for the $45 back, and in its place handed him two $100 bills.

Of the mean, median, mode, and range:

5. Which remained unchanged? ______________________________

6. Which changed? By how much? ______________________________

____

Name ______________________________

Fact or Opinion

There are two kinds of questions you will see when dealing with data of any kind, including questionnaires:

- questions whose answers are facts
- questions whose answers are opinions

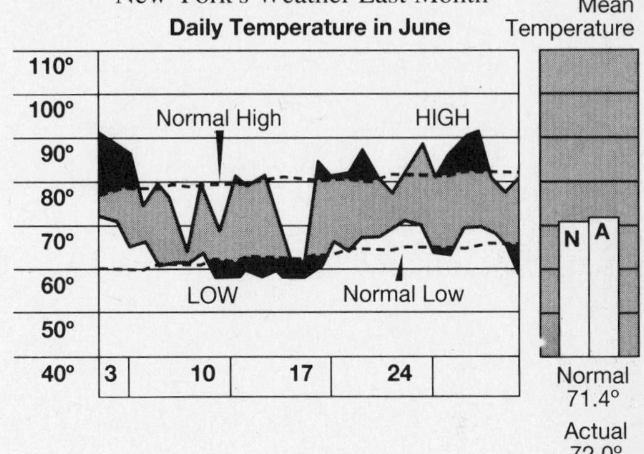

Look at the data in the graphs. For each question below, decide whether the answer would be a fact with which everyone would agree or an opinion that people might disagree with. Write **fact** or **opinion.** You don't have to answer the question.

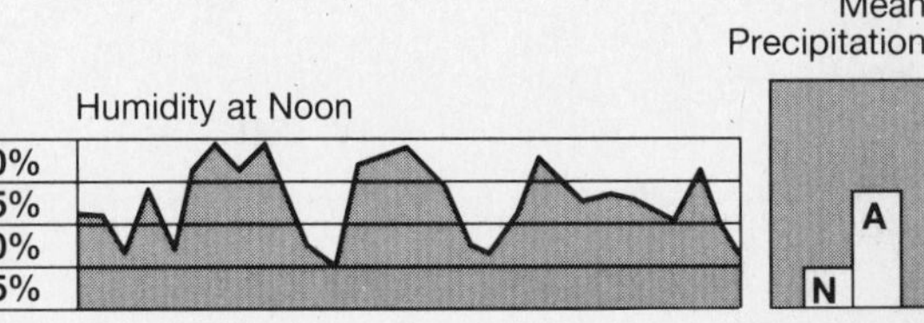

1. Was the actual mean temperature for the month higher than normal? ______________

2. Was the humidity ever below 50%? ______________

3. Was the weather pleasant in New York in June? ______________

4. Did New York get more precipitation (rain) than normal?

____

5. Did New York get more rain than was needed? ______________

6. Is the normal high temperature in June above 85 degrees?

____

7. Is the first or second half of the month nicer? ______________

Name ____

Using a Table

A school supply store advertised this sale:

Shep's Pens at Special Prices! (Tax Included)						
Pens	1	2	3	4	5	6
Price	$0.19	$0.38	$0.57	$0.76	$0.95	$1.14

Use the information in the table to answer these questions.

1. Do you save money on each pen by buying a larger number of pens? Explain.

____

2. Lois thinks she needs 10 pens to start the school year (Lois loves to write!). How can she find the cost of 10 pens without extending the table?

____

____

____

When Shep finds that his pens are not moving as fast as he would like, he reduces his prices. Here is his new ad:

Shep's Pens at Incredible Prices! (Tax Still Included)						
Pens	1	2	3	4	5	6
Price	$0.15	$0.25	$0.40	$0.50	$0.65	$0.75

Use Shep's new ad to answer these questions.

3. When asked to explain his prices, Shep replied, "It's simple.

They're ________ each or 2 for ________." Fill in the blanks.

4. With these new prices, customers flocked to the store. Shep needed to extend the table. How much will 7 pens cost? 8 pens?

____

Name ______________________________

Estimating Sums

You can substitute two pairs of compatible numbers for four of the numbers in each group below to estimate the sum given. Find the pairs. Then write the unused number at the bottom of the page. They will add up to the height of the world's tallest doors.

Example:

Sum: 200

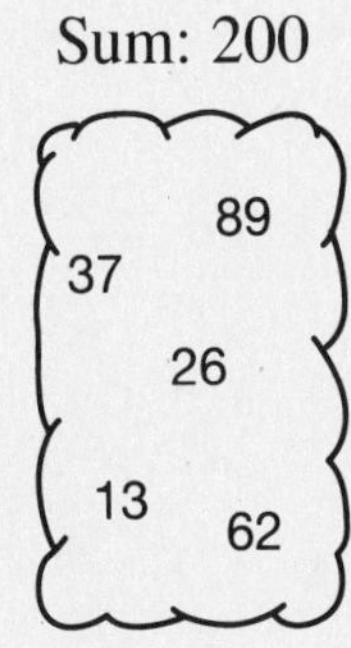

37 + 62 rounds to 40 + 60 = 100
89 + 13 rounds to 90 + 10 = 100
200

26 is extra, but do not include it in the sum below.

1. Sum: 500

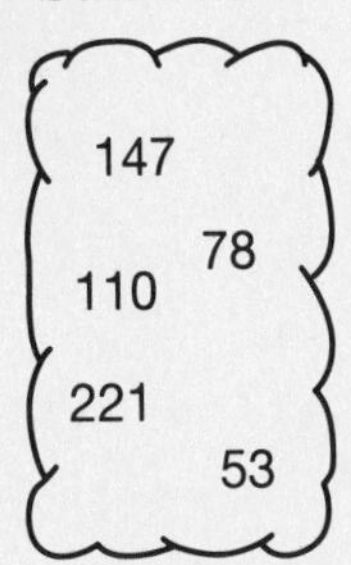

2. Sum: 350

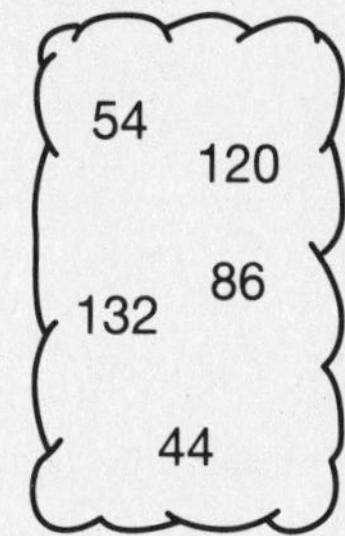

3. Sum: 400

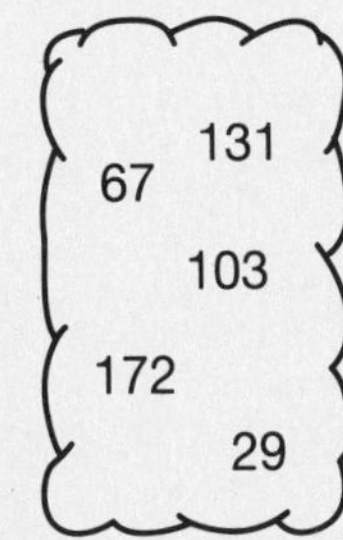

4. Sum: 600

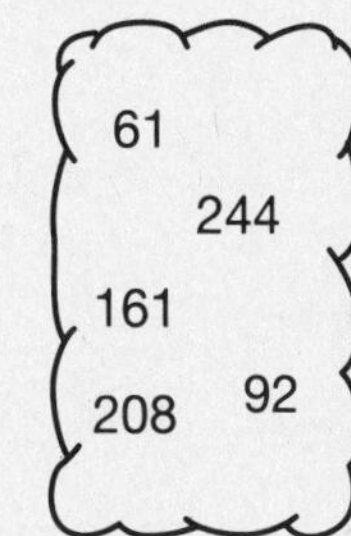

Extra Numbers: ______ + ______ + ______ + ______ = ______
1. **2.** **3.** **4.**

The world's tallest doors are at Cape Canaveral, Florida, and they are ______ feet high.

Name ____

Enough or Not Enough?

The problems on this page contain either more data than you need to solve them or not enough data to solve them.

If there are extra data, use only what you need to solve the problem. If there are not enough data, supply reasonable information and then solve the problem.

1. The Mom and Pop Grocery Store sells juice at $0.49 per container, hamburgers at $1.19, and pretzels at $0.39. If Stanley goes into the store with a $20 bill and buys 1 container of juice, 2 hamburgers, and 1 pretzel, what is the total cost of his purchases?

____

2. While in the store, Stanley discovers that Mom and Pop have back issues of *Retro Man,* his favorite superhero magazine. Does Stanley have enough money left to buy the September, October, and November 1955 issues?

____

3. While Stanley is shopping, his sister Sondra is selling raffle tickets for her Girl Scout troop. So far she has sold 27 tickets. How much has she earned?

____

4. Some people believe that in the year 2086 moon fuel will cost as much as $135 per gallon. The Phelps family will want to make the 240,000-mile, 5-day trip on their vacation. Will 79 gallons be enough fuel if their craft gets 2,817 miles per gallon?

____

5. Rounded to the nearest whole number, about how many gallons of moon fuel will they need to complete a round trip from their home to the lunar surface and back again?

____

Name ______________________

Multiplication Shortcuts

You can use mental math to multiply a number by 5.

Here's how.

Even number: 680 × 5	
Step 1:	Divide the first factor by 2. **680 ÷ 2 = 340**
Step 2:	Multiply the answer by 10. **340 × 10 = 3,400**

Odd number: 681 × 5	
Step 1:	Multiply the first factor by 10. **681 × 10 = 6,810**
Step 2:	Divide the answer by 2. **6,810 ÷ 2 = 3,405**

Find the products. Use mental math.

1. 140 × 5 ______

2. 223 × 5 ______

3. 430 × 5 ______

4. 625 × 5 ______

5. 245 × 5 ______

6. 724 × 5 ______

7. 888 × 5 ______

8. 632 × 5 ______

9. 909 × 5 ______

10. 898 × 5 ______

11. Explain why these shortcuts work. ______

12. Describe shortcuts for multiplying a number by *50*. Explain why they work.

Name ______________________________

Ring the Numbers

The product of one pair of numbers within each sun falls within the given range. Use rounding and mental math to find that pair. Ring them.

1. Range: 200 to 300

2. Range: 400 to 500

3. Range: 700 to 900

4. Range: 900 to 1,200

5. Range: 1,200 to 1,500

6. Range: 2,000 to 3,000

7. Range: 7,000 to 10,000

8. Range: 20,000 to 25,000

Name ______________________________

Another Multiplication Shortcut

You can use mental math to multiply a number by 25.

Here's how.

Multiply 36 by 25.

Step 1: Divide the first factor by 4.
$36 \div 4 = 9$

Step 2: Multiply the answer by 100.
$9 \times 100 = 900$

$36 \times 25 = 900$

Find the products. Use mental math.

1. 16×25 ______________ **2.** 24×25 ______________

3. 48×25 ______________ **4.** 25×80 ______________

5. 25×280 ______________ **6.** 25×160 ______________

7. 360×25 ______________ **8.** 320×25 ______________

9. 25×244 ______________ **10.** 25×84 ______________

11. Explain why the shortcut works.

____

____

12. What must one factor in each exercise have in common to make this shortcut work so well?

____

13. Describe a shortcut for multiplying a number by 250. For multiplying by 20.

____

Name ______________________________

Problems Without Numbers

Read each problem below. Ring the letter of the correct solution method.

1. Mr. Guzzler used a certain number of gallons of gas while driving a certain number of miles. What was the cost of the gas per mile?

A Add the number of gallons to the number of miles. Multiply the result by the price of each gallon.

B Multiply the number of gallons used by the cost per gallon. Divide by the number of miles driven.

C Divide the mileage driven by the number of gallons used. Multiply the result by the price of a gallon.

2. You know the cost of a year's subscription to a monthly magazine and the cost of a copy at the newsstand. How much would you save in a year by buying the subscription?

A Subtract the price of a newsstand copy from the price of a subscription. Divide the result by 12.

B Divide the subscription price by 12. Subtract the result from the price of a newsstand copy.

C Multiply the price of a newsstand copy by 12. Subtract the yearly subscription price from the result.

3. Here are some numbers without a problem. Use these numbers and write your own problem.
47 9 2 5

____

____

Name ________________________________

Squares and More Squares

Solve the problems by first examining simpler cases.

1. How many squares are in the design at the right? ______________

Here are some hints.
First hint: The squares can be different sizes.
Second hint: Use a table. Find the number of squares in a 1×1 square, a 2×2 square, and so on. Look for a pattern.

2. How many squares are in a 6×6 square?

____

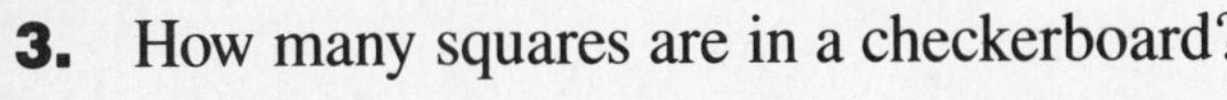

3. How many squares are in a checkerboard?

____

Now try this.

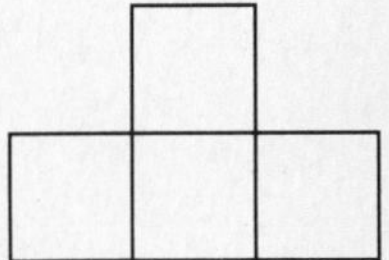

These 4 squares make a block T. Its perimeter is 10.
When 2 block T's are joined as shown, the sum is not 20.

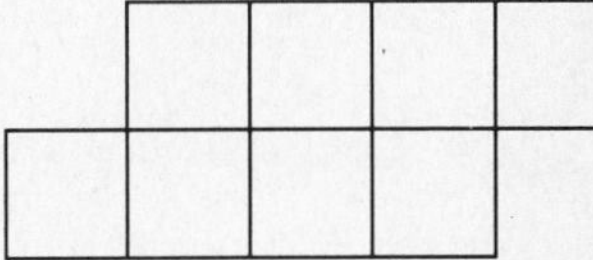

4. What is the perimeter when 10 block T's are joined?

____

5. Describe your strategy. ________________________________

____

Name ______________________________

Breaking Apart Numbers

Complete each statement. Be careful, some are tricky!

1. Multiplying 2 by 53 is the same as multiplying 2 by 50, and 2 by ________, then adding the products.

2. Multiplying 4 by 37 is the same as multiplying 4 by 30, and ________ by 7, then adding the products.

3. Multiplying 3 by 28 is the same as multiplying 3 by 30, and 3 by ________, then ____________________ the products.

4. Multiplying 6 by 97 is the same as multiplying ________ by ________________, and 6 by 3, then subtracting the products.

Complete.

5. $4 \times 83 = (4 \times$ ________$) + (4 \times 3) =$ ________

6. $3 \times 87 = (3 \times 90) - (3 \times 3) =$ ________

7. $7 \times 98 = (7 \times$ ________$) - (7 \times 2) =$ ________

8. $6 \times 55 = (6 \times$ ________$) + ($________ $\times 5) =$ ________

9. $4 \times$ ________ $= (4 \times 30) + (4 \times$ ________$) = 132$

10. $8 \times$ ________ $= (8 \times$ ________$) - (8 \times$ ________$) = 384$

Name ____________________

Tree Minutes and Days

What was the longest time anyone ever spent in a tree? The person who holds the record climbed into a tree house one day and didn't come down for 431 days! Who is this champion tree sitter?

To find out, decide if each product is **less than either factor, greater than both factors,** or **greater than one factor, but less than the other.** Write the letter of your answer above the number for the exercise in the code at the bottom. Use graph paper models to help you decide. For some exercises you may need to use two 10 by 10 squares.

	Less than Either Factor	Greater than Both Factors	In Between the Two Factors
1. 0.7×0.4	T	R	A
2. 0.6×1.1	Y	E	R
3. 0.4×1.3	P	S	O
4. 1.1×1.1	L	T	B
5. 0.8×0.6	O	I	U
6. 1.2×1.3	D	Y	K
7. 0.3×0.9	I	N	E
8. 0.7×0.7	H	J	A
9. 0.7×1.5	T	I	M
10. 0.1×0.1	Y	W	S

___ ___ ___ ___ ___ ___ ___   ___ ___ ___
4   7   9   3   1   8   6   2   5   10

Name ____________________

Talking on the Phone

The table shows telephone rates for calling some towns in Yakkity County from your home in Prattle.

Town Called	9 a.m.–5 p.m. cost per min	5 p.m.–11 p.m. cost per min	After 11 p.m. cost per min
Blabberville	$0.55	$0.45	$0.40
Chatter Hills	$0.48	$0.41	$0.34
Yapper Valley	$0.36	$0.29	$0.22
Blahblah	$0.57	$0.48	$0.42
Gab Creek	$0.31	$0.26	$0.19

Find the cost of each call from Prattle.

1. Call to Yapper Valley at 3:05 p.m., for 5 minutes ________

2. Call to Blahblah at 6:30 p.m., for 7.5 minutes ________

3. Call to Gab Creek at 2:29 p.m., blabbing until 2:45 p.m. ________

4. Call to Chatter Hills after midnight, for 12.7 minutes ________

Solve.

5. A 4-minute call, costing $1.92 was made from Prattle at 9:46 p.m. To which town was the call made? ________________

6. Use the table to make up a problem for classmates to solve.

____

Name ______________________________

What's Cooking at the Video Store?

Muffins, that's what! As Muffin movie madness keeps rising rapidly, people are flocking to their local stores to buy these popular new movies by the batches. They make great holiday gifts.

Use the prices at Mike's Video to solve the problems.

MUFFIN MOVIE SALE

Return of the Muffins	$79.59	Muffin Academy II	$29.95
Muffins of Doom	$51.85	Muffins from Mars	$19.95
High Plains Muffin	$34.59	Muffin Madness	$70.65
Muffinbusters	$12.49	Tarzan and the Muffins	$42.79

1. Phillip spent about $400. He bought 5 copies of one of the videos. Which one?

   ____

2. Dolores bought 2 *Muffins of Doom* videos and 2 copies of another video. She spent about $140. Which other video did she buy?

   ____

3. Nick bought 2 copies of *High Plains Muffin* and 3 copies of another video for a total of about $200. Which other video did he buy?

   ____

4. Hungering for a muffin movie, Yoko bought 2 copies of one video and 5 copies of another. Which did she buy, if she spent about $180?

   ____

   ____

Name ______________________________

Foreign Exchange

Foreign currency exchange rates change every day. The rates appear in the financial pages of newspapers. They tell us how the value of money from other countries compares with the dollar.

The table shows one day's exchange rates.

Country / currency	Rate of Exchange (in dollars)
Great Britain / pound (£)	1.5638
France / france (F)	0.1506
Greece / drachmas (Dr)	0.005963
Hong Kong / dollar (HK$)	0.5025
Spain / pesetas (P)	0.008003

On this day, 1 pound could be exchanged for 1.5638 dollars. Rounded to the nearest cent, that is $1.56. To exchange £20, you would multiply:

$$20 \times 1.5638 = 31.276$$

On this day, £20 could be exchanged for $31.28, to the nearest cent.

Use the table to find equivalent amounts in dollars.
Round your answers to the nearest cent.
You can use your calculator.

1. £30 ________ **2.** 85F ________ **3.** 25HK$ ________

4. 500P ________ **5.** £68 ________ **6.** 1,200Dr ________

7. 138F ________ **8.** 49HK$ ________ **9.** 3,452P ________

10. £16 ________ **11.** 2,384Dr ________ **12.** 103F ________

Name ______________________________

Using Your Calculator's Memory

Dear Family,

Your child has been learning about using a calculator to solve multiple-step problems. Use the information below to write multiple-step problems for each other to solve using a calculator with memory keys. Solve your problem before giving it to the other person.

1. You make a purchase, pay sales tax, then get change from your purchase.

____

____

____

____

2. You have a job for a length of time, in which you are paid by the hour or by the number of items you produce.

____

____

____

____

3. You want to paint a space that requires a certain amount of paint, which is priced differently at different stores.

____

____

____

____

Name ____

Exotic Animal Rentals

Gwen McConner is a movie director who is famous for making films in exotic locations. When she does, she rents rare and unusual animals from Stevie's Species for certain scenes. These special creatures are especially expensive.

Use mental math and the price list to see how Gwen went over budget.

STEVIE'S SPECIES

Giant sloth ....$100 per day
Komodo dragon .... $1,000 per minute
(Who would want one around any longer?)
Blue whale ....$1,000 per week
Giant earthworm ....$100 per minute

Platypus .... $10 per day
White peacock ....$100 per hour
Ostrich ....$10 per minute
Poodle .... $10 per hour
(That dog can really act!)

1. Gwen rented an ostrich for 12.5 minutes. What did it cost?

____

2. Gwen rented a peacock for 24.5 hours and a platypus for half a day. What did she spend?

____

3. Gwen wanted a giant earthworm for a scene that was supposed to take 12.5 minutes. But the dragon ate the camera, and the scene took 3 times as long. What did she have to pay for the earthworm?

____

4. Gwen rented a sloth, a platypus, and a poodle for 2.25 days, and the Komodo dragon for 2.25 minutes. What was the total cost?

____

5. Gwen's budget for creature rental was $8,800. By how much did she exceed her budget?

____

Name ______________________________

Place the Towns

In Wheeler County, Wagon is 10 km south of Gokart. Use this information, the information that follows, and your estimating skills to place the towns on the map.

1. Ferris is about 30 km south of Wagon.

2. Skateboard is about 40 km east of Wagon.

3. Jeep is about 20 km west and 50 km south of Skateboard.

4. Dune Buggy is about 20 km north and 30 km east of Jeep.

5. Stagecoach is about 70 km east of Ferris.

6. Chariot is about 15 km east of Wheelbarrow, which is about 25 km north of Stagecoach.

7. Unicycle is about 15 km south of the halfway point between Dune Buggy and Stagecoach.

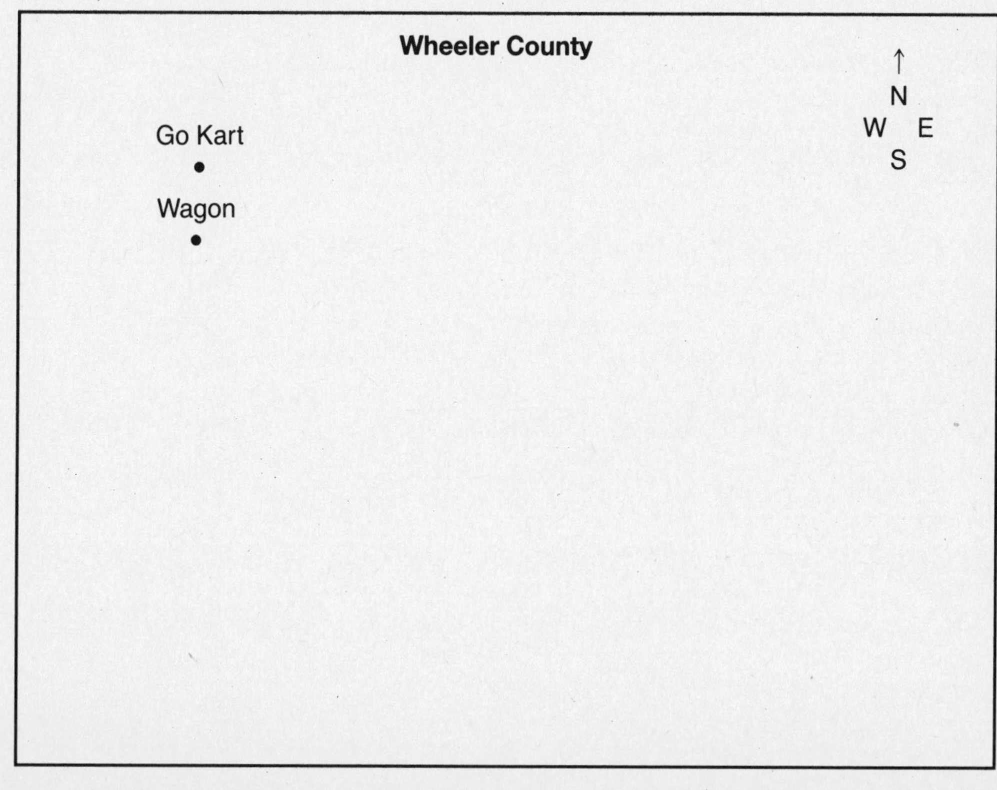

Name ______________________________

Crack the Code

How many lions can a lion tamer tame? Well, the record for feeding and mastering lions by a single trainer is 40 at one time. To find out the name of this brave person, first ring the letter in each row that corresponds to the amount that *does not belong*. Then write that letter above its number at the bottom.

1.	B. 250 cm	Y. 2.5 m	E. 25m
2.	C. 4 m	R. 40 cm	N. 0.4 m
3.	K. 6.72 m	R. 67.2 cm	P. 672 cm
4.	A. 0.83 m	T. 83 cm	E. 8.3 cm
5.	E. 770 cm	J. 0.77 m	I. 77 cm
6.	P. 0.145 m	H. 1.45 cm	L. 14.5 cm
7.	R. 9.2 cm	E. 0.092 m	A. 0.92 m
8.	Y. 4 cm	D. 40 cm	W. 0.04 m
9.	R. 1 m 50 cm	O. 150 cm	L. 15 cm
10.	I. 23 m	J. 2.3 m	K. 230 cm
11.	T. 1 m 6 cm	R. 160 cm	S. 106 cm
12.	M. 234 cm	D. 23 m 4 cm	U. 2 m 34 cm
13.	N. 4 m 93 cm	O. 49.3 m	C. 4,930 cm
14.	D. 10.08 m	S. 108 cm	Y. 10 m 8 cm
15.	B. 717 cm	F. 71 m 7 cm	A. 7 m 17 cm

____ ____ ____ ____ ____ ____   ____ ____ ____ ____ ____ ____ ____ ____ ____

7 9 15 3 4 12   14 2 6 13 1 10 8 5 11

Name ______________________________

Using Meters, Centimeters, and Millimeters

When you work with metric measures, begin by writing them in the same unit. Study the example.

Add: 2 m + 32 cm + 17 mm

Give your answer in centimeters.

2 m = 200 cm   17 mm = 1.7 cm

↓   ↓

200 cm   + 32 cm   + 1.7 cm = 233.7 cm

Add or subtract.

Give your answer in centimeters.

1. 3 m + 29 cm ____________ **2.** 57 cm + 45 mm ____________

3. 4.5 m − 82 cm ____________ **4.** 44 cm − 80 mm ____________

Give your answer in meters.

5. 8.2 m + 25 cm ____________ **6.** 1.42 m − 30 cm ____________

7. 0.7 m − 29 cm ____________ **8.** 0.09 m − 42 mm ____________

Give your answer in either millimeters, centimeters, or meters.

9. 14 cm + 55 mm ____________ **10.** 0.7 m − 26 mm ____________

11. 0.06 m + 0.8 cm + 12 mm ____________

12. 15 mm + 45 cm + 0.5 m ____________

Name ________________________________

Wrapping It Up

Dear Family,

Your child has been learning how to determine the area of a rectangle. There are many ways to model the area of a rectangle to illustrate the concept. One way is by wrapping a package.

Each of the packages below is a rectangular solid—all six faces are rectangles. Together, find the amount of paper needed to wrap each box.

1. 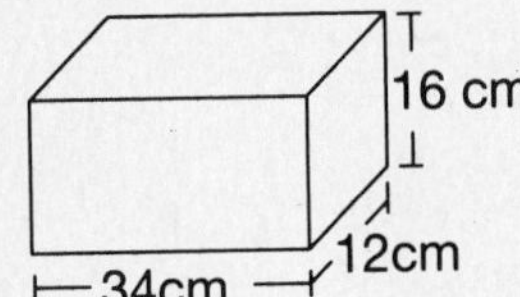

____

2. 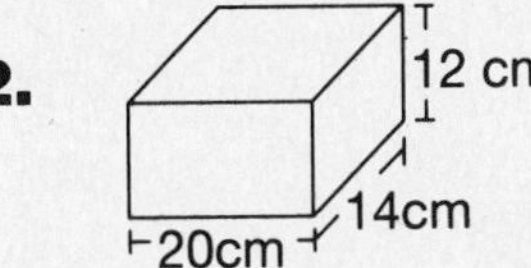

____

3. 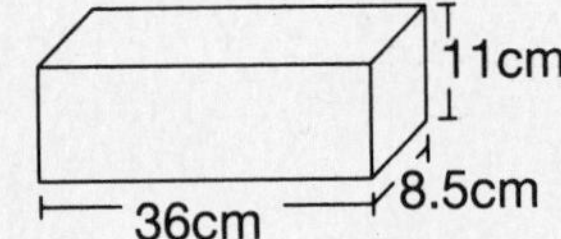

____

4. 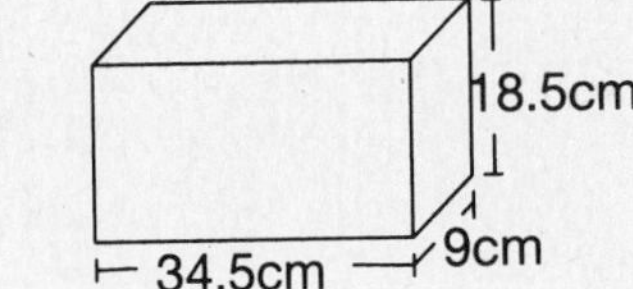

____

5. Explain the method you used to find the total amount of wrapping paper needed for each package. Describe any shortcuts you discovered.

____

6. Estimate the amount of paper needed to wrap a box you have in your house. Then measure the dimensions of the box with a centimeter ruler. Give your estimate and the actual amount of paper needed.

____

Name ______________________________

Estimating Driving Distances

The flying distance from New York City to Chicago is about 1,300 km.
The flying distance from Los Angeles to San Francisco is about 600 km.

Use the information in the map to help you estimate the distances in kilometers and solve the problems.

1. How far is it from Chicago to Denver?

____

2. About how far is the trip from Los Angeles to Dallas?

____

3. Which other distance on the map is about the same as the distance from Los Angeles to Dallas?

____

4. Hank flew from Denver to Dallas. If he flew at an average speed of 800 km per h, including stops, how long did the trip take?
a. 3h b. 30 min c. $1\frac{1}{2}$ h

____

5. A plane leaves Atlanta for Miami at 9:00 a.m. If it averages 800 km per h, about what time should it arrive in Miami?
a. 1:00 pm b.10:15 am c. 12:00 noon

____

Name ______________________________

Estimating Capacity

You will need the following materials:

- a paper cup
- a large glass
- a larger glass or pitcher
- a 1-liter container
- a large pot
- water

1. Estimate how many cups of water will fill the large glass. Write your estimate in the table.

2. Use the cup and the glass to find out the actual amount. Write it in the table.

3. First estimate, then measure the number of cups of water that will fill the larger glass or pitcher, the 1-liter container, and the large pot. Write the results in the table.

	Estimate	Actual
large glass		
larger glass or pitcher		
1-liter container		
pot		

4. How can you use your answer to Question 2 to make the other estimates? To make the other measurements?

____

____

____

Name ____________________

Metric Olympics

How do your skills with metrics measure up? With a group of classmates, enter the Metric Measurement Olympics and find out!

First Event: 10-Meter Walk

Object: To estimate a distance of 10 m

Choose a starting line. Walk until you think you have gone 10 m. Mark the spot with chalk. A student judge measures 10 m from the starting line, using metric measuring tape or a meter stick. Find the distance between your measurement and 10 m. The winner has the estimate closest to 10 m.

1. Repeat the event, each time from a different starting spot. Keep track of your results. Describe them. Are you improving?

____

____

____

____

Second Event: 1-Kilogram Match

Object: To estimate a total mass of 1 kg

Use a plastic bag or a paper bag to gather assorted objects around your classroom. Fill up your bag until you estimate that it has a mass of 1 kg. A student judge will check the bags. The winner has the bag that is closest in mass to 1 kg.

2. Repeat this event, each time filling your bag with different objects. Record your results. Are your estimates getting more accurate? Explain.

____

____

____

____

Name ____

On the Road

Pete is traveling from one city to another, promoting his new book, *It's Easy to Choose.* His book may give good advice, but Pete himself has trouble making up his mind.

1. On the tour he is visiting Pittsburgh, Palo Alto, Portland, and Portsmith. He can't decide in which order to visit them. How many choices does he have?

____

2. A speech Pete has planned has a beginning, a middle, an end, and a time for questions. He knows the questions should come at the end, but can't decide the order of the other parts. How many orders are possible?

____

3. Unable to make up his mind about what to wear, Pete packed his black shoes, his brown, blue, and gray suits, a white shirt, a blue shirt, and a yellow shirt, and a red tie and a striped tie. How many different outfits can he wear if he always wears a tie?

____

4. How many outfits can Pete put together if he decides not to wear his yellow shirt? Or to wear only his white shirt?

____

5. Make up a problem about a daily dilemma Pete faces: ordering breakfast. Then try it out on one of your classmates.

____

____

____

____

Name ______________________________

Meeting Hands

How closely do you watch your watch?
Use a watch with hands, or the clock face on this page.
Ring the time that best describes when the two hands will meet.

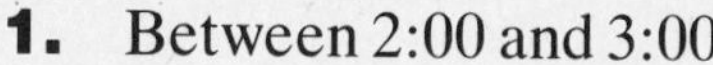

1. Between 2:00 and 3:00

A 2:02 **B** 2:11 **C** 2:20 **D** 2:40

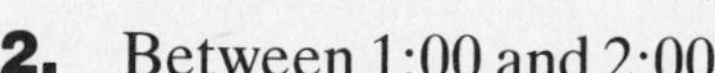

2. Between 1:00 and 2:00

A 1:06 **B** 1:10 **C** 1:30 **D** never

3. Between 11:30 and 12:30

A 11:45 **B** 12:00 **C** 12:12 **D** 12:20

4. Between 8:30 and 9:30

A 8:40 **B** 8:44 **C** 9:00 **D** never

5. Between 2:15 and 3:15

A 2:20 **B** 2:45 **C** 3:03 **D** never

6. Between 5:30 and 6:30

A 5:31 **B** 6:00 **C** 6:29 **D** never

7. Ring the number of times the hands of the clock meet between noon and midnight.

A 6 times **B** 9 times **C** 11 times **D** 12 times

8. Ring the time when the hands of the clock form a straight line.

A 3:15 **B** 9:15 **C** 6:00 **D** 3:45

Name ______________________________

Making Predictions Using a Table

The table gives the average daily high temperatures for some cities around the world in January and in July.

AVERAGE DAILY HIGH TEMPERATURE (°C)		
City	January	July
Athens, Greece	12	32
Bangkok, Thailand	32	32
Buenos Aires, Argentina	29	14
Cairo, Egypt	18	36
Istanbul, Turkey	7	27
Moscow, U.S.S.R	⁻6	24

Use the information in the table to answer the questions.

1. In which city is it colder in July than in January?

____

2. It is the middle of January and the temperature has dropped to ⁻8°C. In which city is this most likely to have happened?

____

3. It is July and the temperature in your city is about 5°C warmer than in Moscow. In which city do you probably live?

____

4. It is the end of January and it is unusually cool for the city you are in. The temperature has dropped to 21°C. In which city (or cities) might you be?

____

5. You can save money by living in this city because you can wear the same clothing all year round. Which city is this?

____

 Use with text pages 170-171.

Name ______________________________

Quick and Easy

Presto Donefast likes to make math quick and easy. He always looks for patterns and rules. Use patterns to solve the division problems. Then write which one of Presto's rules describes how the pattern in each group works.

Presto's Rules		
Rule A	Rule B	Rule C
The quotient doubles when the dividend doubles and the divisor remains the same.	The quotient is halved when the dividend remains the same and the divisor is doubled.	The quotient is halved when the divisor remains the same and the dividend is halved.

1. 36 ÷ 9 = ____ 360 ÷ 9 = ____ 3,600 ÷ 9 = ____

2. 36 ÷ 18 = ____ 360 ÷ 18 = ____ 3,600 ÷ 18 = ____

3. 36 ÷ 36 = ____ 360 ÷ 36 = ____ 3,600 ÷ 36 = ____

4. 36 ÷ 72 = ____ 360 ÷ 72 = ____ 3,600 ÷ 72 = ____

Rule: ____

5. 144 ÷ 9 = ____ 1,440 ÷ 9 = ____ 14,400 ÷ 9 = ____

6. 72 ÷ 9 = ____ 720 ÷ 9 = ____ 7,200 ÷ 9 = ____

7. 36 ÷ 9 = ____ 360 ÷ 9 = ____ 3,600 ÷ 9 = ____

8. 18 ÷ 9 = ____ 180 ÷ 9 = ____ 1,800 ÷ 9 = ____

9. 9 ÷ 9 = ____ 90 ÷ 9 = ____ 900 ÷ 9 = ____

Rule: ____

Name ______________________________

Souvenirs Here!

Last summer Tony T shirt sold souvenirs at outdoor concerts. The table below shows how many times each group performed and each group's total souvenir earnings. Estimate to the nearest hundred to complete the table. Then solve the problems.

Group	Performances	Total Earnings	Estimated Earnings per Show
Boots Without Laces	8	$5,783	______
Etched Brass	6	$5,078	______
The Torn Tapes	5	$1,114	______
WE NO!	9	$8,418	______
Street at Dawn	3	$1,937	______

1. Which group had the highest earnings per show? ______

2. Which group brought in the least per show? ______

3. What group's per-show earnings were roughly equivalent to the combined per-show earnings of The Torn Tapes and Street at Dawn? ______

4. Next year WE NO! is scheduled for 15 concerts. If their souvenirs continue to sell at the same rate, about how much can Tony expect their total earnings to be? ______

Name

Pail of Peanuts

Frances was frantic. She had volunteered to divide up the prizes from the Pail of Peanuts Party before she realized she had not yet learned the division she would need. Then she had an idea. Look at how Frances approached the division for the first pail. Then use her method to solve the remaining problems.

1. 72 peanuts shared by 3 winners

$$\begin{array}{r} 60 \div 3 = 20 \\ +12 \div 3 = +4 \\ \hline 72 \div 3 = 24 \end{array}$$

2. 84 peanuts shared by 4 winners

3. 96 peanuts shared by 8 winners

4. 81 peanuts shared by 3 winners

5. 65 peanuts shared by 5 winners

6. 84 peanuts shared by 7 winners

7. 56 peanuts shared by 4 winners

8. 48 peanuts shared by 4 winners

9. 78 peanuts shared by 6 winners

10. 60 peanuts shared by 5 winners

Name ______________________________

Match the Quotients

The quotients of two of the division problems in each group are the same. Use reasoning and mental math to identify the two problems without dividing. Then ring the matching problems.

1. $6\overline{)540}$ $3\overline{)270}$

$6\overline{)1080}$ $3\overline{)1080}$

2. $8\overline{)136}$ $4\overline{)136}$

$8\overline{)68}$ $4\overline{)68}$

3. $8\overline{)288}$ $4\overline{)288}$

$4\overline{)576}$ $8\overline{)576}$

4. $8\overline{)402}$ $2\overline{)402}$

$4\overline{)402}$ $8\overline{)804}$

5. $1\overline{)115}$ $6\overline{)345}$

$3\overline{)345}$ $1\overline{)345}$

6. $4\overline{)114}$ $8\overline{)228}$

$2\overline{)228}$ $2\overline{)114}$

7. $6\overline{)150}$ $6\overline{)75}$

$3\overline{)150}$ $3\overline{)75}$

8. $8\overline{)464}$ $4\overline{)464}$

$2\overline{)232}$ $4\overline{)928}$

9. $8\overline{)124}$ $4\overline{)124}$

$4\overline{)248}$ $8\overline{)248}$

10. $6\overline{)108}$ $6\overline{)216}$

$3\overline{)216}$ $3\overline{)54}$

Name ____________________

Catalog Confusion

Samantha works for the Earth Gifts Catalog Company. She just received the order below. As you can see, Dizzy sent his money, but he forgot to write *what* he wanted. Samantha thinks she could figure out what Dizzy had in mind, but she does not have time. Help her out. Use the catalog page at the right to complete Dizzy's order.

EARTH GIFTS	
Cosmic Calendar	$13.00
Fish Mobile	$17.00
Hummingbird Feeder	$11.00
Indoor/Outdoor Thermometer	$45.00
Lizard Pin	$15.00
Lunar Tie	$35.00
What T-Shirt	$19.00
Wind Chimes	$65.00

Send to: Dizzy Didrush
342 Dapple Street
Wayward, TN

Description	Quantity	Price Each	Total
	9		$153.00
	5		175.00
	7		77.00
	8		120.00
	3		195.00
	6		270.00
	9		171.00
	8		104.00

Total Payment Enclosed ____________

Name ______________________________

More than Meets the Eye!

Students at Greenpoint Elementary would be astonished at the truth. Mrs. Dodgson, the math teacher, is a famous criminal detective. The answers on the chalkboard are actually a coded signal telling the police where the notorious Fairweather Gang is hiding out. You can unlock the code! Use a calculator to match each quotient expressed as a whole number and decimal with the equivalent quotient at the bottom of the page. Write the letters of the matching quotients in the blanks.

A 7,375 ÷ 8 = 921.875

D 7,374 ÷ 8 = 921.75

E 5,517 ÷ 6 = 919.5

G 4,606 ÷ 5 = 921.2

H 7,373 ÷ 8 = 921.625

L 3,688 ÷ 4 = 922.0

N 4,611 ÷ 5 = 922.2

O 3,682 ÷ 4 = 920.5

R 4,609 ÷ 5 = 921.8

T 5,541 ÷ 6 = 923.5

___ 921 R1 ___ 921 R4 ___ 921 R7 ___ 922 R1 ___ 921 R6

___ 921 R5 ___ 920 R2 ___ 923 R3 ___ 919 R3 ___ 922

Name ______________________________

Averages

Dear Family,
Your child has been learning how to find averages. You can plan a family project that will help show how people can use averages in their daily lives.

First, talk about why averages are useful. Is one test score or an average of several scores more representative of a student's work? Why are batting averages used in baseball?

Next, discuss how each of you spends free time. Keep a record, like the one below, of time spent on leisure activities.

	Shooting Baskets	Reading	TV/Movies	Making Models	Biking
Monday					
Tuesday					
Wednesday					
Thursday					
Friday					
Saturday					
Sunday					
Weekly Average					

At the end of the week discuss whether you are surprised at the results. Do you spend more or less time than you thought on certain activities? Are there ways either of you would want to change your schedules so that you did more of what you like most?

Name ______________________________

Blast Off!

Anita is the president of the Model Rocket Club. She is thinking about the year ahead. Following is the list of questions she must answer before she can complete her plans. Can you answer them for her?

1. The club has budgeted $185.00 for rockets. New rockets with launchers cost $33.85. If Anita buys 4 rockets with launchers, will there be funds left over to buy rockets alone? If so, how many $12.00 rockets could Anita buy? ____________

2. The club budgeted $116 for rocket engines. Each package costs $3 and contains 3 engines. How many packages can Anita buy and how many engines will she get? ____________

3. Ralph has a 90-cm length of balsa wood left over from last year. How many fin pieces can be cut from this length if each fin requires 11 cm? ____________

4. A package of 6 igniters costs $2. How many packages can the club purchase for $33, and how many igniters will they get? ____________

5. Each table at the club has room for 4 people to work. How many tables are needed for the 27 club members? ____________

6. Anita estimates that a Pegasus rocket will require 10 hours of work to complete. How many days would it take to complete a Pegasus if a member could work $1\frac{1}{2}$ hours per day? ____________

7. Each launching requires about 20 minutes from countdown to recovery. Only one rocket can be launched at a time. If the club has 7 members per week ready to launch, will it be sufficient to schedule 2 hours per week on the launching field? ____________

Name ______________________________

What Is My Number?

Pandora loves tricky problems. She made these up for the Math Fair. How many can you solve?

1. One half of my number added to one third of 33 is the same as 2 less than the product of 7 and 9. What is my number? ________

2. If you double my number, you will have one half the number of hours in 2 days. What is my number? ________

3. Take the product of twice 10 and one half of my number. Divide it by 4. You will get 25. What is my number? ________

4. You can easily find my number if you follow these simple steps. Multiply one more than thrice 33 by one less than one fifth of 55. Double the result and add 1. What is my number? ________

5. I am thinking of a number that is the same as the double of one fourth of 28. What is my number? ________

6. Rachel found my number by multiplying the number of days in a week by the number of eggs in a half-dozen carton, but Sebastian preferred to find the sum of one half of 80 and 2. What is my number? ________

7. If you subtract my number from 99, not once and not twice, but 8 times, you will get 19. What is my number? ________

8. If you divide my number by 8 and then multiply the result by one half of eight, you will get 16. What is my number? ________

9. One fifth of my number subtracted from 26 is the same as one third of 72. What is my number? ________

Name ______________________________

Unit Pricing

Stores frequently sell items in groups. Consumers can compare costs by finding the unit price, or the cost of one item. Each problem below gives 4 costs. Estimate the unit price for each. You will find that 3 of the unit prices are about the same. Ring the cost that represents the *different* unit price.

1. 8 for $4.81   10 for $6.19
9 for $8.20   6 for $3.75

2. 10 for $29.89   9 for $26.05
4 for $11.95   6 for $12.19

3. 6 for $80.00   3 for $76.03
4 for $102.00   2 for $49.72

4. 3 for $350.00   2 for $142.00
5 for $351.19   7 for $489.22

5. 5 for $41.86   6 for $55.24
7 for $58.45   3 for $25.00

6. 7 for $36.06   6 for $32.04
8 for $41.27   2 for $101.49

7. 2 for $0.25   9 for $1.10
3 for $3.65   4 for $0.50

8. 5 for $4.60   4 for $3.59
3 for $3.60   9 for $8.22

9. 3 for $147.13   8 for $40.00
9 for $448.17   6 for $305.13

10. 6 for $54.95   7 for $49.00
2 for $19.19   4 for $37.18

Name ____

Marsha's Mosaics

Marsha creates mosaic patterns for her customers. She just received a new shipment of tiles. When she looked at the packing slip, she realized it gave only the perimeters of the tiles. Marsha needed to know the length of the sides as well. The packing slip is shown below. Use the measurements given to find the length of one side for each type of tile Marsha received.

		Perimeter	Side
1.	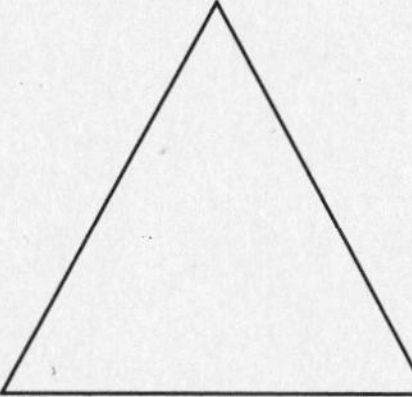	10.05 in.	________
2.		18.52 in.	________
3.	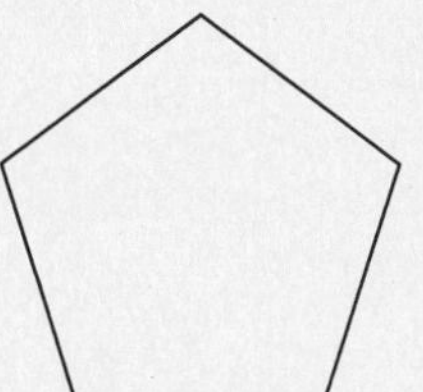	26.25 in.	________
4.	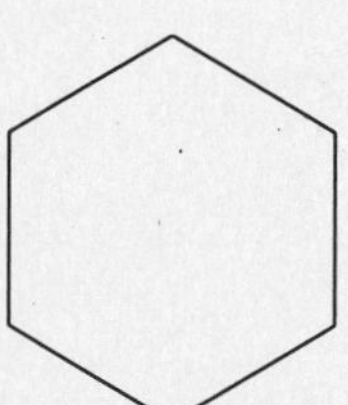	24.75 in.	________
5.	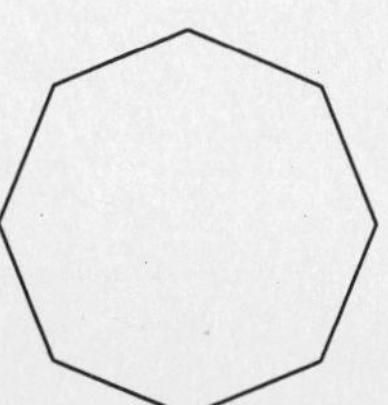	49.6 in.	________

Name ____

Ask Abacus

Abacus is on vacation. His editor has the letters for this week's "Dear Abacus" column. However, Abacus has left two responses for each, and the editor is confused. Help her out. Choose the response that is mathematically reasonable and put a check by it.

1. Dear Abacus,
I buy gas for my car about 4 times a month. I pay $0.89 per gallon, and my tank holds about 16 gal. The gas station just sent my monthly bill — $569.60!! Could this be true?

______ Yes, it could. Do you need a better paying job?

______ No way. It looks to me like someone was charging you $8.90 a gallon. That's pretty steep!

2. Dear Abacus,
I bought a chest of drawers at Home Stores' One-Day Half-Price Sale. It cost $329.00 regularly. They charged me $16.45. Am I dreaming?

______ Yes, you're dreaming, but Home Stores better wake up. Somebody took half off $32.90.

______ No, you're not dreaming. One half of $329 has been $16.45 since the last leap year.

3. Dear Abacus,
I need 2,500 25-cent stamps, but the post office wants to charge me $625. That seems like too much money to pay for a bunch of stamps. What should I do?

______ Politely explain to your postmaster that he needs a new calculator.

______ If you're not willing to pay for postage, then deliver your letters by hand.

4. Every time we go to the store my brother and I argue over the peanut butter. He says the 12-oz jar for $1.49 is a better buy. I say the $1.79 18-oz jar is cheaper. We can never agree. We have not bought any peanut butter in 6 months, and I miss it. Tell us he's wrong. Please!

______ This is a silly argument. Just do the division. You'll see that the 12-oz jar is cheaper!

______ This is a silly argument. Just do the division. You'll see that the 18-oz jar is cheaper!

Name ______________________________

Making Changes

Whenever you change months to years, you *divide* by 12.

12 months = 1 year   24 months = 2 years

Whenever you change years to months, you *multiply* by 12.

3 years = 36 months   5 years = 60 months

Decide what number you would multiply or divide by to make the change described.

1. Change dimes to pennies. ______________________

2. Change nickels to dollars. ______________________

3. Change weeks to days. ______________________

4. Change years to decades. ______________________

5. Change half-days to hours. ______________________

6. Change minutes to days. ______________________

7. Change half-centuries to decades. ______________________

8. Change quarters to $5 bills. ______________________

9. Change yards to inches. ______________________

10. Change football games to quarters. ______________________

Use with text pages 212-213.

Name ______________________________

The Happy Camper

Uncle Jack Bluelake owns 6 sleep-away camps. His ad shows the prices for a 1-week stay at each campsite.

Uncle Jack Provides the Best in Camping

BE SURE TO RESERVE YOUR WEEK EARLY!

Camp	Jack's low price
Bugbite	$149.95
Muckabout	$202.50
Underbush	$ 95.50
Takeahike	$420.95
Homesick	$256.00
Wannaleave	$ 62.50

Use your estimation skills and the information in the ad to name each camp described.

1. Five campers signed up. The parents paid a total of $312.50.

____

2. Seven campers signed up. The parents paid a total of $1,417.50

____

3. Six campers signed up. The parents paid a total of $2,525.70.

____

4. Twenty campers signed up. The parents paid a total of $1,910.00.

____

5. Ten campers were signed for 1 week each, and ten for 2 weeks each. The parents paid a total of $6,075.00.

____

Name ____________________

Loading Little Leaguers

Every year Little Leaguers from different towns go on a trip to see a Major League baseball game. They go to the game by bus and by van. Use the information in the table to solve the problems about how they get there.

Little League	Number of Players
Capstown	227
Homer Valley	84
Batborough	188
Gloversville	76
Fieldston	151
Moundsburgh	242

1. One town needs four 48-seat Basset buses to take their players. There is room for 4 adults, too. Which town is it?

____

2. Stan's vans can hold 15 Little Leaguers. How many vans are needed to take the entire Gloversville group to the game?

____

3. If this town delivers its players in 6 of Jan's 14-seat vans, there is no room for any adults. Which town faces this problem?

____

4. All Snail buses have 52 seats. If Capstown goes by Snail, how many buses will they need if they also want to bring along about 30 parents?

____

5. If this town uses the Basset Bus line, it will have to find a way to get 7 players to the game or hire another bus. Which town is it?

____

Name ______________________________

Find the Answers

In each exercise, one of the answers is correct. Use estimation and number sense to find it. Then solve the problem to check your estimate.

1. 378 ÷ 54 = ________ 6 7 8

2. 298 ÷ 37 = ________ 6 R2 7 R2 8 R2

3. 459 ÷ 76 = ________ 6 R3 7 R3 8 R3

4. 390 ÷ 48 = ________ 7 R6 8 R6 9 R6

5. 417 ÷ 56 = ________ 7 R25 8 R29 9 R24

6. 772 ÷ 81 = ________ 7 R45 8 R44 9 R43

7. 375 ÷ 63 = ________ 5 R60 6 R12 7 R4

Estimate to ring all the numbers that would make each statement true.

8. 243 ÷ 48 is greater than ________ 3 4 5 6 7 8

9. 557 ÷ 73 is greater than ________ 5 6 7 8 9

Name ______________________________

Egyptian Division

The ancient Egyptians divided by using doubles. Here is how they would have divided 400 by 37.

First they made a table of doubles for the divisor, 37.

They stopped at the first product greater than 400.

greater than 400

$1 \times 37 = 37$
$2 \times 37 = 74$
$4 \times 37 = 148$
$8 \times 37 = 296$
$16 \times 37 = 592$

Then they subtracted some of the doubles, starting with the greatest double less than 400.

Next they subtracted the largest double they could and so on.

$$\begin{array}{r l} 400 & \\ -\ 296 & \leftarrow \mathbf{8} \times 37 \\ \hline 104 & \\ -\ 74 & \leftarrow \mathbf{2} \times 37 \\ \hline 30 & \end{array}$$

Finally they added the numbers by which 37 was multiplied.

$$\mathbf{8 + 2 = 10}$$

$400 \div 37 = 10$ R30

Divide by using the Egyptian doubling method. Check your answers by dividing your usual way.

1. $24\overline{)227}$

2. $59\overline{)827}$

3. $43\overline{)2{,}000}$

Name ____

Creating Problems for Others

Use the information in the table to make up problems for your classmates to solve according to the directions below. Problems can involve any operations. Give the solutions to your problems.

Aurora's Audio Outlet

Title	Price
Rabbits Hum their Favorites	$25
Sounds of the Oceans	$12.50
Star Trip XII: The Tape	$75; 3 for $195
Arctic Noises	$12 for $204
The World's Scariest Stories	$15; 20 or more for $9.95 each
The Best of the Dinosaur Singers	$155

Write two problems that can be solved using mental math.

1. ____

____

2. ____

____

Write two problems that you would need either a calculator or pencil and paper to solve.

3. ____

____

4. ____

____

Write one 2-step problem for which you would use both a calculator and mental math to solve.

5. ____

____

Name ______________________________

Missing Digits

Write the missing digits in the boxes.

1.

```
         ☐☐☐ R☐☐
  29)11, 6 1 2
   - 11 6
       0 1 2
     -   0 0
         ☐☐
```

2.

```
            ☐☐ R1
  34) 2 , 2 4 5
     -☐  0 4
         ☐☐5
       - 2 0☐
             1
```

3.

```
          2 ☐ 5 R☐☐
  ☐4 6) 9 , 4 4 8
       -☐ 2
          2 4
        -   0
          2 4 8
        -☐☐☐
           ☐☐
```

4.

```
           8 ☐☐ R☐☐
  2☐) 1 9, 6 5 4
     -☐9 ☐
         4 5
       -☐☐
         2 1 4
       -☐☐☐
           2 2
```

5.

```
          8 ☐ R☐
  3☐)☐, 2 ☐ 7
     - 3 1 2
       1 5 7
     -☐☐☐
           ☐
```

6.

```
            5 ☐ R3☐
  ☐☐)☐, ☐☐☐
      - 3 1 0
        2 7 ☐
      -☐☐☐
         ☐ 1
```

Name ______________________________

Sports Patterns

Each of the problems below can be solved using one or more of the problem solving strategies you have been learning. What they all have in common is that each involves recognizing a pattern.

1. Sally hits a home run at the rate of one every 3 days. Kevin hits home runs at the rate of one every 5 days. Walt hits one every 12 days. All three sluggers hit a home run today. When is the next time all three will hit homers on the same day? When is the time after that?

____

2. Jenny scored a total of 135 points in 5 games. Each game she scored 2 more points than in the previous game. How many points did she score in the 5th game?

____

3. Ali is a very steady scorer for her team. She always scores 9 points. In 9 games she would score 81 points. In 99 games, 891 points. How many points will she score in 9,999,999 games? HINT: Begin by figuring out how many points in 999 games.

____

4. In a single-elimination tournament, if you lose once, you are out of the competition. How many games are played in a 5-player single-elimination chess tournament? In a 10-player tournament? In an 864-player tournament?
HINT: Use smaller numbers and look for a pattern.

____

Name ______________________________

Developing Decimal Number Sense

Use mental math to write >, <, or = in the ◯ to make the number sentence true. Check your answers with a calculator.

1. 8×10 ◯ $8 \div 0.1$

2. $14 \div 0.01$ ◯ $14 \div 0.1$

3. 5×100 ◯ $5 \div 0.001$

4. $2.4 \div 0.1$ ◯ 2.4×100

5. $23 \div 0.1$ ◯ $2.3 \div 0.1$

6. 6.8×0.001 ◯ $6.8 \div 1{,}000$

7. $0.1 \div 0.1$ ◯ 0.1×0.1

8. $200 \div 1{,}000$ ◯ 20×0.01

Round the divisor in each problem below to 10, 100, or 1,000, whichever makes sense. Next, use mental math to estimate the quotient. Then write > or < to tell whether your estimate is less than or greater than the exact answer. Finally, use a calculator to find the answer rounded to three decimal places.

	Estimate	> or <	Calculated Answer
9. $83.2 \div 9.8$			
10. $243 \div 1{,}004$			

Name ____________________

Not Enough Gas

Dear Family,

Your child has been learning to use estimation to solve problems. Together, solve the estimation problems below. Use the information in the map. Ring the best answer.

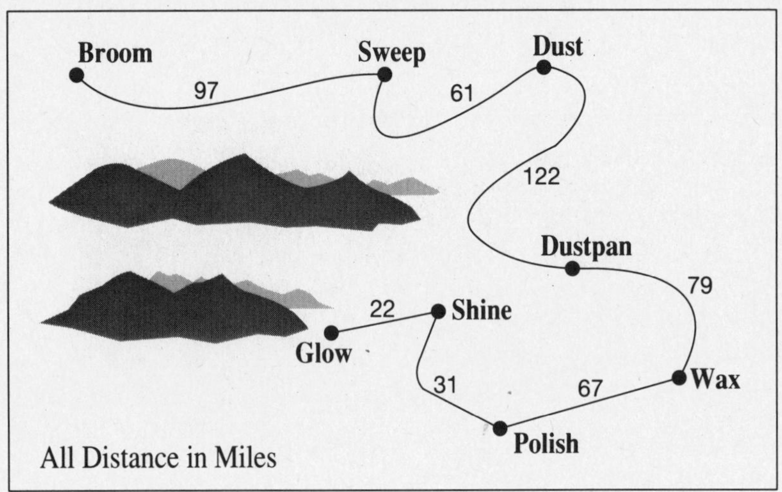

Ring the best answer.

1. Bill left Broom with 15 gallons left in his gas tank. He ran out of gas just short of Dust. His car gets about — 10 mpg — 15 mpg — 30 mpg

2. Sabrina drove from Sweep toward Shine with 12.2 gallons of gas in her tank. She ran out of gas about 25 miles past Polish. Her car gets about — 20 mpg — 30 mpg — 40 mpg

3. Gladys left Glow with 10.95 gallons in her tank. She ran out of gas as she pulled into Dust. Her car gets about — 25 mpg — 30 mpg — 35 mpg

4. Shelley's car has a gas tank that holds 15 gallons. She drove from Glow to Broom. Before leaving on this trip, she had already used 2.9 gallons of gas. Her car ran out of gas as she got to Broom. Her car gets about — 30 mpg — 35 mpg — 40 mpg

Name ______________________________

Fractional Figures

Divide each figure into the smallest number of equal parts needed to show the given fraction. Then shade the fractional part named.

1. $\frac{1}{2}$

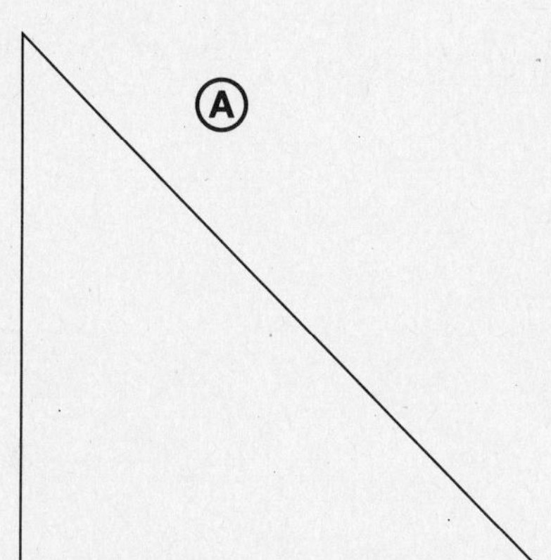

2. $\frac{3}{4}$

3. $\frac{1}{3}$

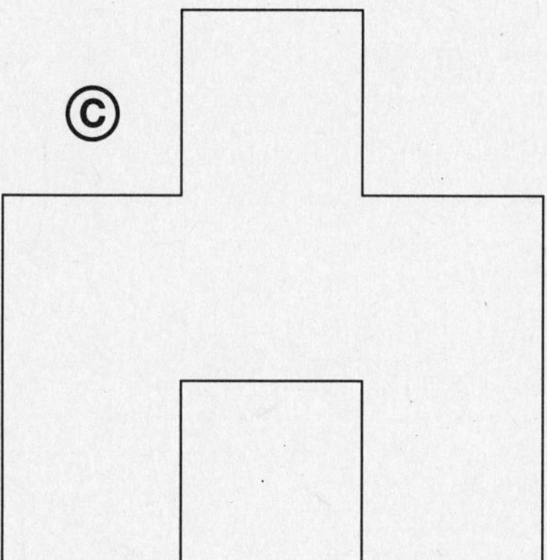

4. $\frac{5}{6}$

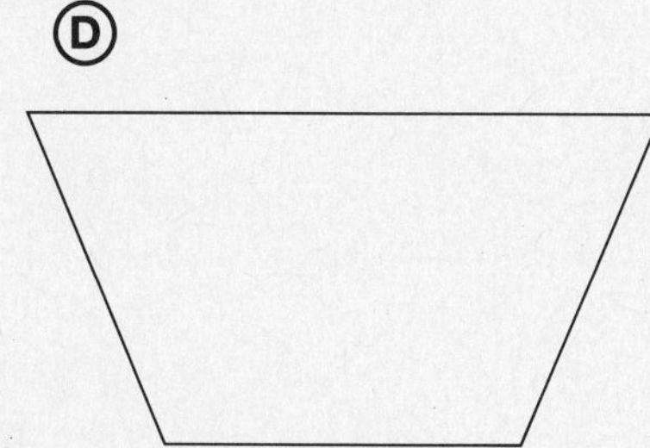

5. $\frac{1}{5}$

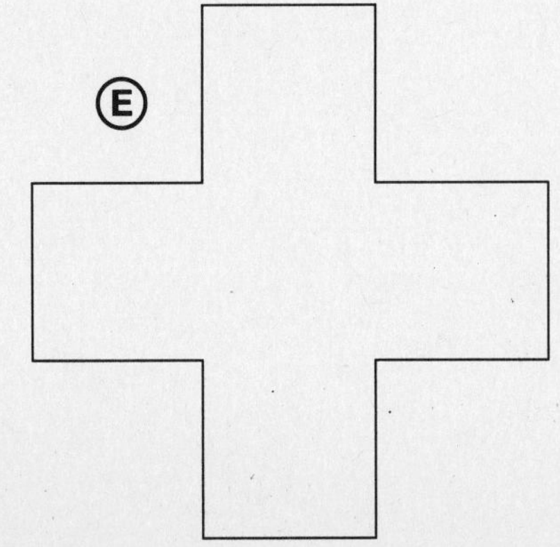

6. $\frac{1}{4}$

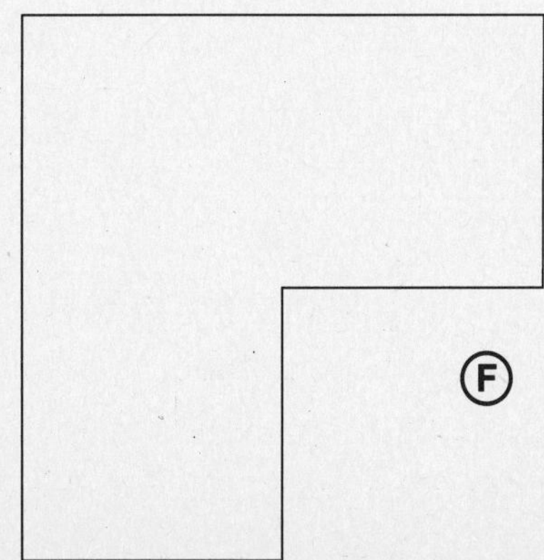

Name ______________________________

Swap Shop

Mr. I. L. Redeemit runs a business (which makes very little profit). Customers bring items to Mr. Redeemit's shop to exchange for items of equal value. For this service, Mr. Redeemit charges a small fee. However, sometimes he is careless and allows customers to make exchanges in which the items are not of equal value.

Here are some exchanges made recently. Decide whether the items exchanged were of equal value. Write **yes** or **no.** Use the illustrations to help you.

1. Rhonda brought in a carton that was $\frac{3}{5}$ filled with books. Mr. Redeemit gave her a carton the same size as the one she brought in, but $\frac{6}{10}$ filled. ______

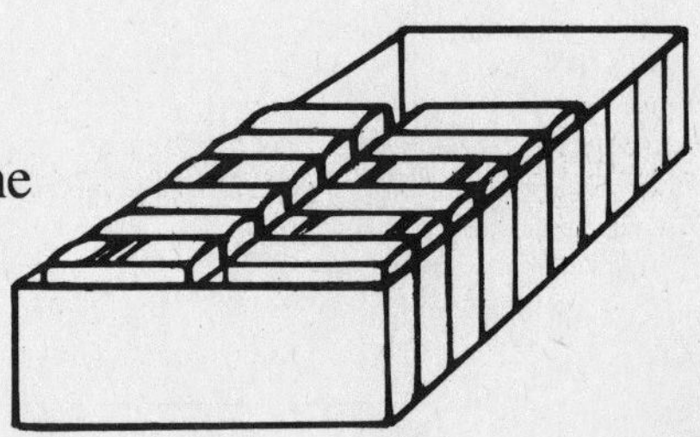

2. George had a quart container of milk that was still $\frac{1}{2}$ full. Mr. Redeemit gave him another quart container that was $\frac{5}{8}$ full. ______

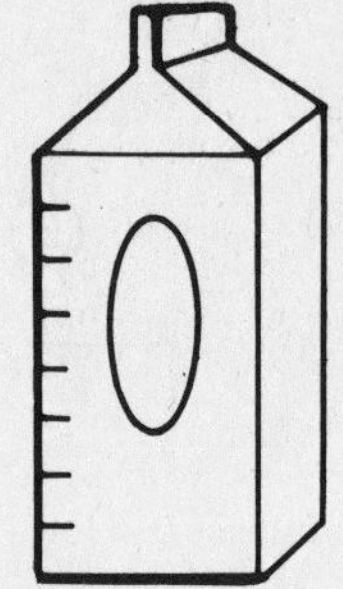

3. Jennifer came in with an egg carton that contained 5 eggs. In its place, Mr. Redeemit gave her one with $\frac{1}{3}$ dozen eggs.

______

4. Alex was unhappy with the flavor toothpaste he was using. He brought in the tube, which was still $\frac{4}{5}$ full. Amazingly, Mr. Redeemit had the same size in a different flavor. It was $\frac{8}{10}$ full. ______

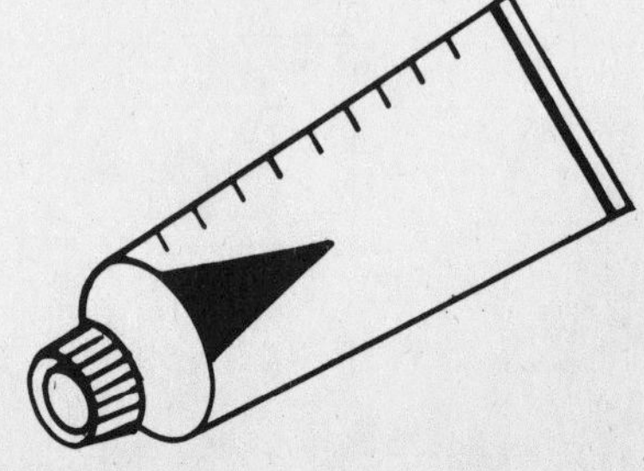

Name ______________________________

Equivalent Fractions

You can find equivalent fractions using a calculator.

For example, to find a fraction equivalent to $\frac{3}{5}$:

- Decide on a denominator for the equivalent fraction. Let's say you choose 25.
- Write the equation: $\frac{3}{5} = \frac{?}{25}$
- Use your calculator. Divide 3 by 5, then multiply by 25.

  Press [3] [÷] [5] [×] [2] [5] [=].

- The result is the numerator of the equivalent fraction, in this case: $\frac{3}{5} = \frac{15}{25}$.

However, if the result on your calculator is a decimal number, there is no equivalent fraction with whole numbers using that denominator.

For example: $\frac{3}{4} = \frac{?}{9}$

[3] [÷] [4] [×] [9] [=] 6.75

- Decimal number, try a different denominator.

Use your calculator to find the equivalent fractions.

1. $\frac{2}{8} = \frac{}{32}$ **2.** $\frac{4}{10} = \frac{}{30}$ **3.** $\frac{9}{12} = \frac{}{36}$ **4.** $\frac{1}{9} = \frac{}{36}$

Is there an equivalent fraction with the denominator shown? Use your calculator to decide. Write the fraction if there is one, or **no** if there is not.

5. $\frac{3}{8} = \frac{?}{30}$ ______ **6.** $\frac{7}{10} = \frac{?}{49}$ ______ **7.** $\frac{5}{9} = \frac{?}{36}$ ______ **8.** $\frac{4}{7} = \frac{?}{28}$ ______

Name ____________________

A New Class

A new class is to be formed. There will be a different number of boys than girls in the class. The teacher has agreed to allow girls to sit only with other girls and boys only with other boys. However, every table in the room must have the same number of students. Working with the teacher, the students decide that the largest number of boys or girls that can possibly be at any table is 3. How many boys and girls can be in the class? List all the possible combinations if you know that there are more than 30 students but fewer than 40.

Work with a partner. Use different color chips or counters for boys and girls to help you decide what the possible combinations are.

When you have listed all the possible combinations, use these clues to decide on the actual number of boys and girls.

- The total of boys and girls is an even number.
- There are exactly 6 more girls than boys. ____________________

 Use with text pages 246-247.

Name ______________________________

Fractions in the Multiplication Table

Did you know that the multiplication table shown here is full of equivalent fractions, many of them in lowest terms?

For this activity, you will need: a copy of the table and a pair of scissors.

Cut the part below and to the right of the double lines into horizontal strips. The first two will look like this:

X	1	2	3	4	5	6	7	8	9	10
1	1	2	3	4	5	6	7	8	9	10
2	2	4	6	8	10	12	14	16	18	20
3	3	6	9	12	15	18	21	24	27	30
4	4	8	12	16	20	24	28	32	36	40
5	5	10	15	20	25	30	35	40	45	50
6	6	12	18	24	30	36	42	48	54	60
7	7	14	21	28	35	42	49	56	63	70
8	8	16	24	32	40	48	56	64	72	80
9	9	18	27	36	45	54	63	72	81	90
10	10	20	30	40	50	60	70	80	90	100

1	2	3	4	5	6	7	8	9	10

2	4	6	8	10	12	14	16	18	20

By placing any strip directly above another, you will form a set of equivalent fractions. The two strips above show the fraction $\frac{1}{2}$ and nine other names for it.

Use the strips to find the lowest terms for each of these fractions. If the fraction is already in lowest terms, write **LT.** Be careful. Some of the fractions can be made from strips in which the first fraction is not in lowest terms.

For example:

4	8	12	16	20	24	28	32	36	40
10	20	30	40	50	60	70	80	90	100

$\frac{8}{20} = \frac{4}{10}$, but $\frac{4}{10}$ is not in lowest terms.

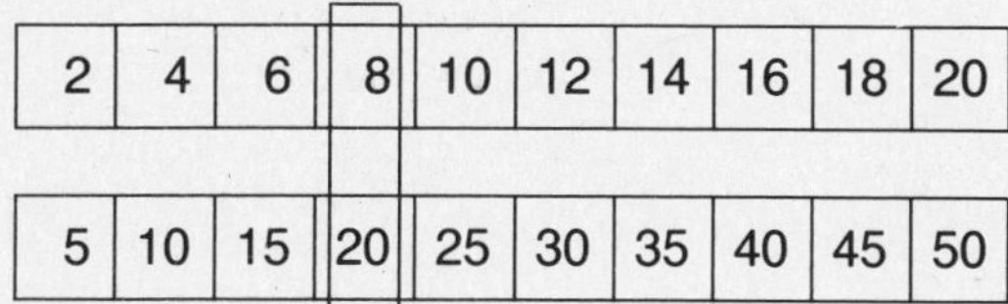

2	4	6	8	10	12	14	16	18	20
5	10	15	20	25	30	35	40	45	50

$\frac{8}{20} = \frac{2}{5}$; $\frac{2}{5}$ is in lowest terms.

1. $\frac{18}{27}$ ______ **2.** $\frac{2}{9}$ ______ **3.** $\frac{25}{30}$ ______ **4.** $\frac{42}{60}$ ______

5. $\frac{21}{56}$ ______ **6.** $\frac{15}{24}$ ______ **7.** $\frac{3}{10}$ ______ **8.** $\frac{14}{49}$ ______

Name ______________________________

Number Patterns

Look at this series of numbers and at the way they are drawn.

1 3 6 10 15

The numbers 1, 3, 6, 10, 15 . . . are called **triangular numbers**.

What will be the next triangular number after 15? __________

If the distance between 2 points is 1 unit, what is the perimeter

(the distance around the outside) of the triangle above the 3? __________

Complete this table:

triangular number	1	3	6	10				36
perimeter of drawing	0	3	6	9	12			

What is the pattern for the top row? For the bottom row?

____

____

There is also a series called **square numbers.**

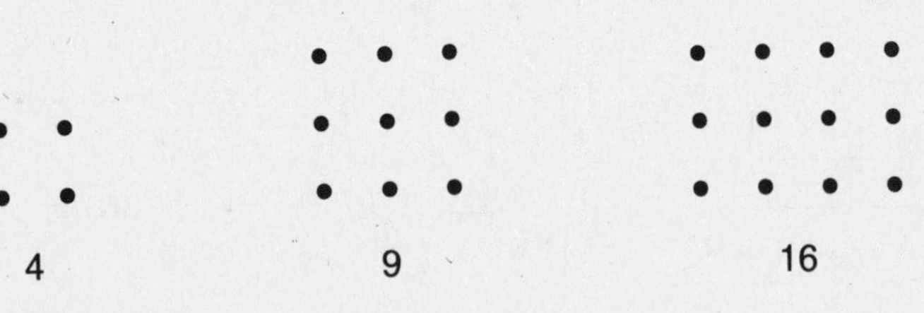

1 4 9 16 25

What will be the next number in this series? __________

Make a table for square numbers.

What is the pattern for the top row? For the bottom row?

____

____

Name ______________________________

Think Logically

Use logical reasoning to solve these different types of problems.

In these problems, each letter stands for a different digit. Find the value of each letter.

1.

```
     A A A
+        M
----------
 M , I I I
```

2.

```
   T A R
 + R A T
 -------
   E E E
```

3.

```
   O P E N
 + W I D E
 ---------
   A A A A
```

Solve for each mystery number.

4. I am a number between 60 and 90. I am a multiple of both 4 and 7. Who am I?

____

5. I am a multiple of 5. I have 2 digits. The sum of my digits is 13. Who am I?

____

6. My tens digit is 3 times my ones digit. My hundreds digit is 2 times my tens digit. My thousands digit is equal to my tens digit. Who am I?

____

Name ______________________________

Redeemit's Swap Shop: The Sequel

Since we last visited Mr. Redeemit, he has added a new service to those he performs for his customers. For a slightly larger fee than that which he charges for other services, Mr. Redeemit will allow you to exchange an item for a larger amount of the same item.

For example, if you brought in an old book that had only $\frac{2}{5}$ of its pages, you could exchange it for a copy of the same book that still had $\frac{1}{2}$ of its pages. You could make the exchange because $\frac{1}{2} > \frac{2}{5}$.

Suppose you had a large carton filled with the stuff described below. Which of the following exchanges would get you a larger amount at Redeemit's?

	Would you exchange . . .	For . . .
1.	a shoe with only $\frac{2}{3}$ of its heel	the same shoe with $\frac{7}{9}$ of its heel? ______
2.	$\frac{3}{4}$ of an anchovy pizza	$\frac{3}{8}$ of another anchovy pizza? ______
3.	$\frac{1}{4}$ lb of your favorite vegetable, turnips	$\frac{3}{10}$ lb of the same yummy veggie? ______
4.	a BMX tire with $\frac{5}{8}$ of its spokes	a newer tire with $\frac{8}{12}$ of its spokes? ______
5.	$\frac{5}{9}$ kg of your best fish tank gravel	$\frac{1}{2}$ kg of the same glorious gravel? ______

Name ______________________________

Geoboard Areas

Use a geoboard and rubber bands to experiment with possible solutions in this activity. Then draw your solutions on geoboard or dot paper.

block

$\frac{1}{3}$ $\frac{1}{3}$ $\frac{1}{3}$

On a geoboard, you can decide to let any area represent one unit. For example, we can say that this rectangle has an area of 1 block unit. Since the rectangle has 3 equal sections, we can also say that the area is $\frac{3}{3}$ block units. To draw a figure with an area of $1\frac{1}{3}$ or $\frac{4}{3}$ block units, we need to add one more section. Here is one figure whose area is $1\frac{1}{3}$ block units. Can you draw another one?

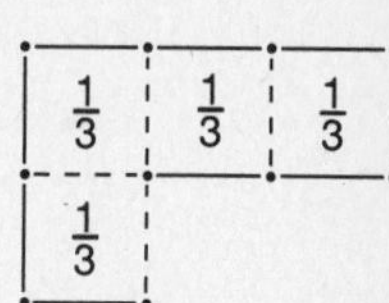

Follow this model to solve the problems below.

1. Assume that the area of this figure is 1 brick unit or $\frac{2}{2}$ brick units. Draw a figure whose area is $1\frac{1}{2}$ brick units.

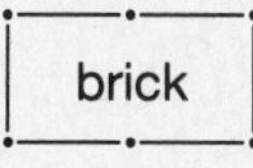

2. Assume that the area of this figure is 1 el unit. Draw a figure whose area is $1\frac{1}{4}$ or $\frac{5}{4}$ el units.

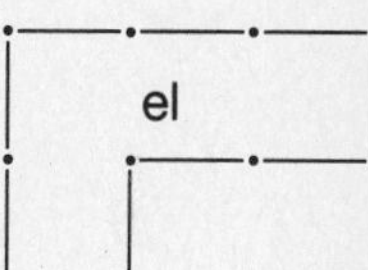

3. Assume that the area of this figure is 1 tile unit. Draw a different figure whose area is 1 tile unit.

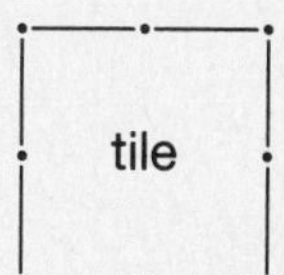

4. Assume that the area of this figure is 1 or $\frac{5}{5}$ floor units. Draw a figure whose area is $1\frac{2}{5}$ or $\frac{7}{5}$ floor units.

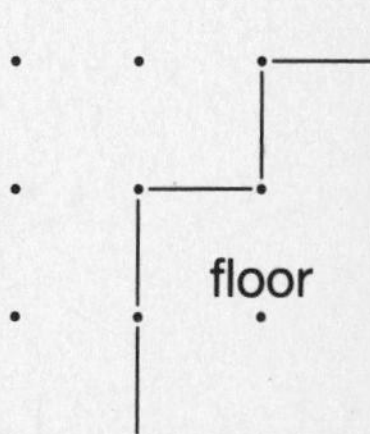

5. Assume that the area of this figure is 1 or $\frac{8}{8}$ rug units. Draw a figure whose area is $1\frac{1}{2}$ or $\frac{12}{8}$ rug units.

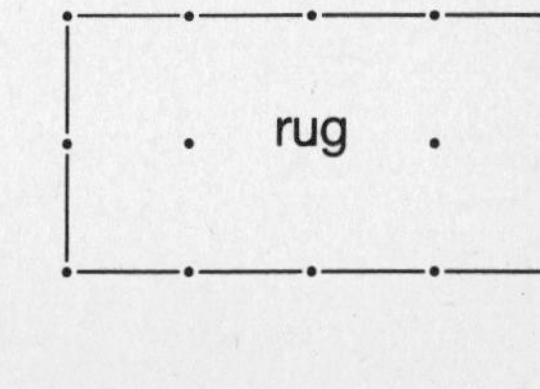

Name ____________________

A Safe Path

World-famous adventurer Stanley Livingstone studied these river rocks long and hard to discover a safe path across. He finally realized that the only stones that would not collapse under his weight were the ones that formed the only path on which every number is larger than the one he stepped on previously.

What path did Stan take if he jumped only horizontally or vertically, never diagonally?

Name ______________________________

Labels with Tables

The labels below are from popular cereals. Call them Cereal H, Cereal K, and Cereal O. Use the information to answer the questions.

Cereal H

NUTRITION INFORMATION PER SERVING
SERVING SIZE........1 OUNCE (APPROX. 1 CUP)
SERVINGS PER PACKAGE....................8

	1 oz.	+ ½ cup vitamin A & D fortified skim milk
CALORIES	100	140
PROTEIN, g	3	7
CARBOHYDRATE, g ...	23	29
FAT, g..............	1	1
CHOLESTEROL, mg ...	0	0
SODIUM, mg	240	300
POTASSIUM, mg	110	310

PERCENTAGE OF U.S. RECOMMENDED DAILY ALLOWANCES (U.S. RDA)

PROTEIN	4	10
VITAMIN A..........	100	110
VITAMIN C..........	100	100
THIAMIN	100	100
RIBOFLAVIN.........	100	110
NIACIN.............	100	100
CALCIUM	20	35
IRON	100	100
VITAMIN D..........	10	25
VITAMIN E..........	100	100
VITAMIN B_6.........	100	100
FOLIC ACID	100	100
VITAMIN B_{12}........	100	110
PHOSPHORUS	15	30
MAGNESIUM	8	10
ZINC..............	100	100
COPPER	6	6
PANTOTHENIC ACID ..	100	100

Cereal K

NUTRITION INFORMATION PER SERVING
SERVING SIZE: 2/3 cup (1 ounce, 28.3g)
SERVINGS PER BOX: 18

	1 oz.	With ½ cup Skim Milk**
Calories	90	130
Protein	3 g	7 g
Carbohydrate	23 g	29 g
Fat	1 g	1 g
Cholesterol	0 mg	0 mg
Sodium	0 mg	60 mg

PERCENTAGE OF U.S. RECOMMENDED DAILY ALLOWANCES (U.S. RDA)

	1 oz.	With ½ cup Skim Milk**
Protein	4	15
Vitamin A	*	4
Vitamin C	*	*
Thiamine	4	8
Riboflavin	*	10
Niacin	8	8
Calcium	*	15
Iron	4	4
Vitamin D	*	15
Phosphorus	10	25
Magnesium	8	10
Zinc	4	8
Copper	6	8

*Contains less than 2% of the U.S. RDA of these nutrients.

Cereal O

NUTRITION INFORMATION PER SERVING
SERVING SIZE.............1 OUNCE (1 ¼ CUPS)
SERVINGS PER PACKAGE..................10

	1 ounce	plus ½ cup vitamin A & D fortified skim milk
CALORIES	110	150
PROTEIN, g	4	8
CARBOHYDRATE, g	20	26
FAT, g	2	2
CHOLESTEROL, mg	0	0
SODIUM, mg	290	350
POTASSIUM, mg ...	105	310

PERCENTAGE OF U.S. RECOMMENDED DAILY ALLOWANCES (U.S. RDA)

PROTEIN	6	15
VITAMIN A........	25	30
VITAMIN C........	25	25
THIAMIN..........	25	30
RIBOFLAVIN.......	25	35
NIACIN	25	25
CALCIUM	4	20
IRON.............	45	45
VITAMIN D........	10	25
VITAMIN B_6	25	30
FOLIC ACID	25	25
PHOSPHORUS	10	20
MAGNESIUM	10	15
ZINC.............	6	8
COPPER	6	6

1. Which cereal box provides the largest number of servings?

____

2. If your cereal bowl held exactly one cup, which cereal would not fit in the bowl?

____

3. How many calories does $\frac{1}{2}$ cup skim milk add to each cereal?

____

4. How many grams of fat are there in $\frac{1}{2}$ cup of skim milk?

____

5. Which cereal provides the largest percentage of calcium?

____

6. How many servings of Cereal O with skim milk would you need to get 100% of daily recommended calcium?

____

Name ______________________________

A Piece of Pizza

Hiram makes only two kinds of pizza in his store: Special Pizza and Very Special Pizza. Use the information about Hiram's pizzas to solve the problems. Give your answers in lowest terms.

Hiram's Special Pizza—10 slices

$\frac{2}{5}$ of the slices have only mushrooms	$\frac{1}{5}$ have only onions
$\frac{1}{5}$ have only peppers	$\frac{1}{5}$ have only anchovies

1. What fraction of the pizza has either mushrooms or peppers? ______

2. What fraction has no onions? ______

3. What fraction has neither anchovies nor mushrooms? ______

Hiram's Very Special Pizza—12 slices

$\frac{1}{12}$ of the slices have only sausage	$\frac{4}{12}$ have only eggplant
$\frac{2}{12}$ have only peppers	$\frac{2}{12}$ have only onions
$\frac{3}{12}$ have only mushrooms	

4. What fraction of the pizza has either peppers or eggplant? ______

5. What fraction has neither mushrooms nor onions? ______

6. What fraction has either sausage, eggplant, or mushrooms? ______

7. Carl ate two of the eggplant slices and a slice with onions on it. What fraction of the remaining pizza is either mushroom or pepper?

______

Name ______________________________

In Between

You can always find a fraction between any two fractions.

Here's how: Find a fraction between $\frac{1}{3}$ and $\frac{3}{5}$.

Rewrite the fractions with a common denominator.

$\frac{1}{3} = \frac{5}{15}$

$\frac{3}{5} = \frac{9}{15}$

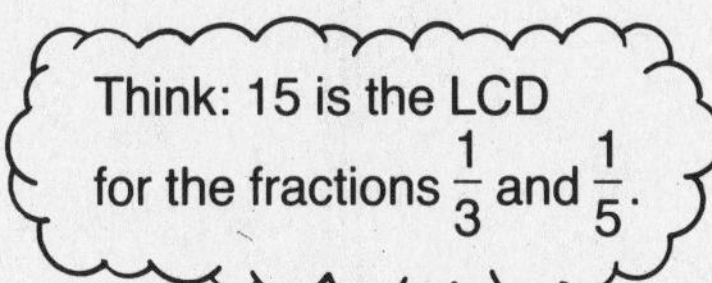

Choose a fraction between the two new fractions.

$\frac{6}{15}$, $\frac{7}{15}$, and $\frac{8}{15}$ are all between $\frac{1}{3}$ and $\frac{3}{5}$.

Find a fraction between each pair of fractions.

1. $\frac{3}{8}$ and $\frac{5}{8}$ ______

2. $\frac{1}{5}$ and $\frac{1}{3}$ ______

3. $\frac{1}{6}$ and $\frac{3}{8}$ ______

4. $\frac{2}{3}$ and $\frac{1}{4}$ ______

5. $\frac{1}{2}$ and $\frac{5}{6}$ ______

6. $\frac{3}{5}$ and $\frac{3}{4}$ ______

7. Explain how you would find a fraction between two fractions whose denominators are the same and whose numerators are 1 apart, such as $\frac{6}{8}$ and $\frac{7}{8}$?

____

____

Find a fraction between each pair.

8. $\frac{4}{7}$ and $\frac{5}{7}$ ______

9. $\frac{5}{8}$ and $\frac{6}{8}$ ______

10. Choose any two fractions that are not equivalent fractions. How many fractions can you find that fall between them?

____

Name ______________________________

At the Old Seaport

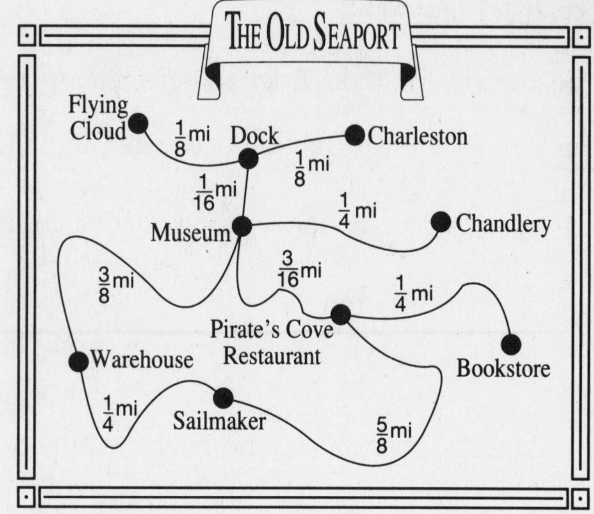

The fifth graders at the Shore School are visiting the restored Old Seaport. They gathered at the dock before dividing into groups to explore the port. Use the map to answer the questions.

1. One group walked to the *Flying Cloud* and to the *Charleston,* then returned to the dock. How far did they walk?

____

2. A second group visited only one of the ships, then went to the museum before returning to the dock. Compare the distance they walked with the distance the first group walked.

____

3. Another group started from the museum, stopped at the warehouse, the sailmaker, and Pirates' Cove Restaurant before returning to the museum. How much farther than a mile was their walk?

____

4. A fourth group started from the dock and took the shortest route to the bookstore. How far was their walk?

____

5. Toward the end of the day, one group was at the sailmaker's shop when a member realized it was time to return to the dock. What is the shortest route back to the dock?

____

Name ____________________

In the Water

Natalie and Gloria swim every day. They record their distances in a table.

Distances in Miles					
	Monday	Tuesday	Wednesday	Thursday	Friday
Natalie	$\frac{1}{10}$	$\frac{1}{6}$	$\frac{1}{8}$	$\frac{1}{4}$	$\frac{1}{2}$
Gloria	$\frac{1}{5}$	$\frac{1}{6}$	$\frac{3}{8}$	$\frac{1}{3}$	$\frac{3}{8}$

Use the table to solve the problems.

1. How far did Natalie swim on Monday and Tuesday? ____________

2. How far did Gloria swim on Tuesday and Wednesday? ____________

3. On Monday, how much farther than Natalie did Gloria swim? ____________

4. On which day did the two girls swim the shortest combined distance? The longest combined distance? ____________

5. On which day did they swim a total of half a mile? ____________

6. On which day did Gloria swim $\frac{1}{12}$ mile farther than Natalie? ____________

7. Who swam farther on Monday and Tuesday? How much farther? ____________

8. Who swam farther on Thursday and Friday? How much farther? ____________

Name ______________________________

Solutions Without Problems

All the solutions below have problems. For each solution, use the digits given, fraction bars, and either a plus sign or a minus sign to name its problem.

1. Solution: $\frac{1}{3}$
Use the digits 3, 4, 6, and 1. $\frac{4}{6} - \frac{1}{3}$

2. Solution: $\frac{5}{8}$
Use the digits 8, 2, 1, and 1. __________

3. Solution: $\frac{1}{2}$
Use the digits 3, 8, 12, and 2. __________

4. Solution: 1
Use the digits 6, 4, 3, and 8. __________

5. Solution: $\frac{2}{3}$
Use the digits 1, 5, 15, and 3. __________

6. Solution: $\frac{1}{4}$
Use the digits 6, 9, 12, and 3. __________

7. Solution: $\frac{1}{8}$
Use the digits 16, 6, 6, and 3. __________

Name ______________________________

A Slice of the Pie

> Dear Family,
> Your child has been learning how to estimate fraction sums and differences. The two of you can solve these problems together.

At the end of a rough rugby tournament, four of the teams stormed into Peg's Pizza Parlor for a light lunch.

Peg will sell only whole pizzas, no slices. A large pie contains 8 slices, and a small pie has 6 slices. Each team huddled. Each totaled the number of slices it wanted and gave its results, as fractions of pizzas, to Peg.

The Dandelions ordered $1\frac{2}{3}$ small sausage pizzas, 1 small onion and pepper pizza, $1\frac{1}{2}$ large mushroom pizzas, and $1\frac{7}{8}$ large cheese pizzas.

The Lambs ordered $\frac{2}{3}$ of a small sausage, 1 large mushroom, $1\frac{1}{6}$ small onion and pepper, and $1\frac{1}{8}$ large cheese.

The Muffins wanted $1\frac{1}{6}$ small sausage, $\frac{3}{4}$ of a large mushroom, $1\frac{1}{4}$ large cheese, and $\frac{2}{3}$ of a small onion and pepper.

The Bunnies ordered 1 small onion and pepper, $1\frac{1}{2}$ large cheese, 1 small sausage, and $1\frac{1}{4}$ large mushroom.

How many of each kind of pizza should Peg make?

1. small sausage ______

2. large mushroom ______

3. small onion and pepper ______

4. large cheese ______

Name ____________________

A Carpentry Project

Read the story. Then write what you see or what is happening on the line below each step.

While building a set of cabinets, carpenters discovered that they had 2 long planks of wood. They wanted to use $1\frac{1}{4}$ planks. Here is what they did to find the amount that was extra.

Step 1:

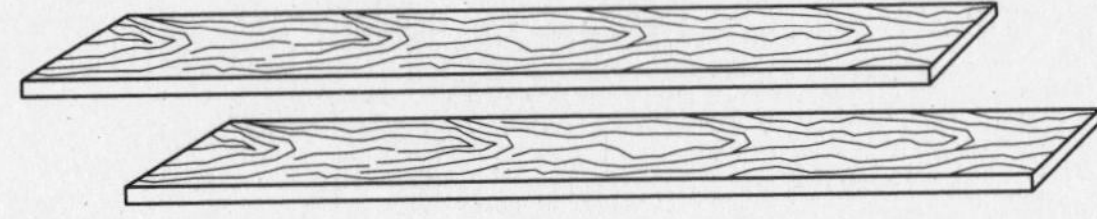

____

____

Step 2:

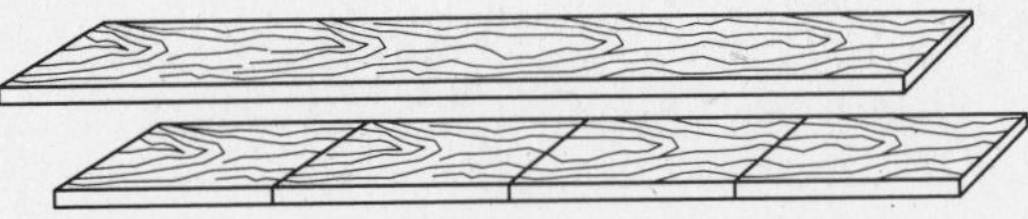

____

____

Step 3:

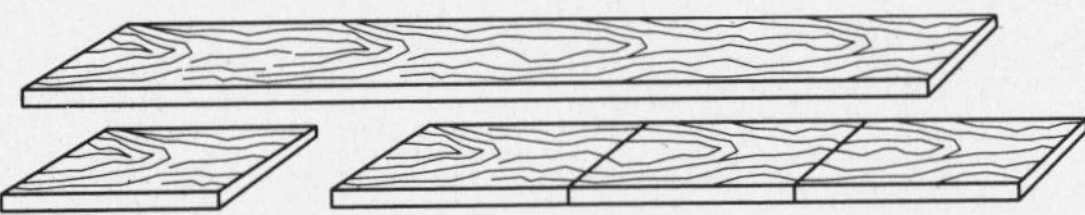

____

____

Step 4:

____

Now describe the story by completing the fraction problem:

$$\begin{array}{r} 2 \;= \\ -\,1\frac{1}{4} = \\ \hline \end{array}$$

Name ______________________________

Addition Clues

Choose fractions or mixed numbers from the box that correctly fit each description. Use numbers as often as you need them.

$1\frac{5}{6}$	$2\frac{1}{8}$	$\frac{3}{4}$	$3\frac{3}{10}$	$\frac{7}{8}$
$2\frac{1}{4}$	$\frac{9}{10}$	$\frac{1}{2}$	$3\frac{1}{6}$	

1. Two numbers whose sum is $2\frac{7}{12}$. ______________________

2. Three numbers whose sum is $4\frac{7}{10}$. ______________________

3. Two numbers whose sum is between 4 and $4\frac{1}{4}$.

____

4. Two mixed numbers and a fraction whose sum is $5\frac{1}{8}$.

____

5. Four numbers whose sum is less than 4.

____

Now make up a story problem to fit each description.

Name ______________________________

Say Cheese

At a country market, you can buy a wheel of cheddar cheese (a complete circle) or a fraction of a wheel.

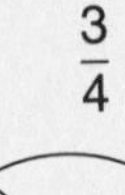
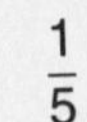

1 whole wheel	$\frac{3}{4}$	$\frac{2}{3}$	$\frac{1}{2}$	$\frac{2}{5}$	$\frac{1}{3}$	$\frac{1}{4}$	$\frac{1}{5}$

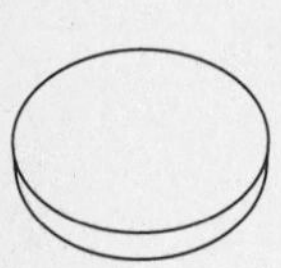

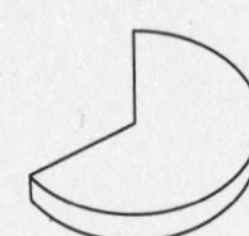

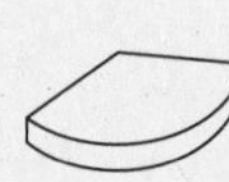
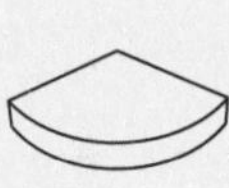

Look at the cheeses ready to be weighed on the balance scales. Which scales will balance? Write the amount of cheese that will be placed on each side of the scale. If the scale will balance, write **B** on it. If not, write the amount of cheese that will make the scale balance on the side where it is needed.

1.

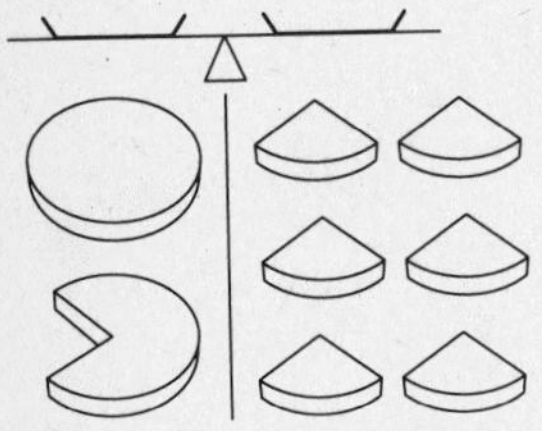

Amount ________ Amount ________

4.

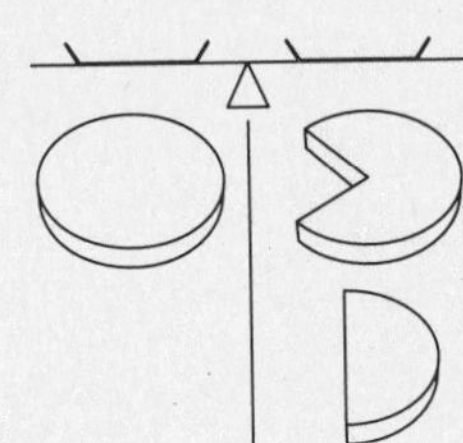

Amount ________ Amount ________

2.

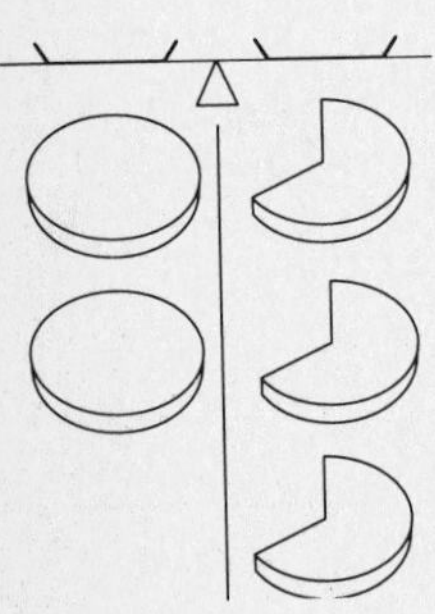

Amount ________ Amount ________

5.

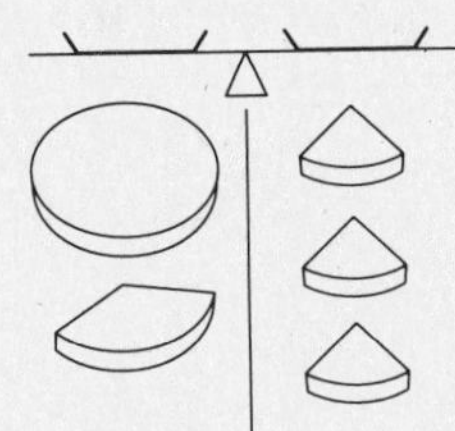

Amount ________ Amount ________

3.

Amount ________ Amount ________

6.

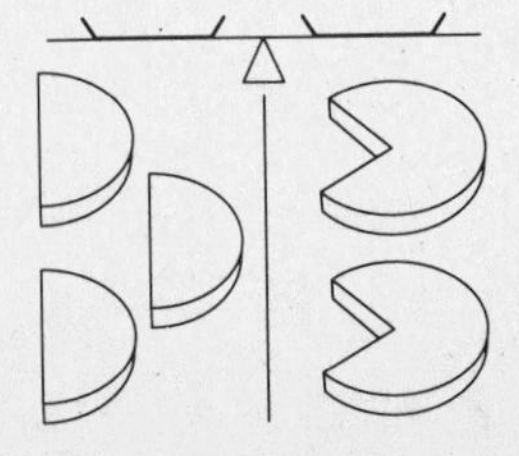

Amount ________ Amount ________

Name ______________________________

Domino Math

You can think of dominoes as pictures of fractions. Each part of the domino can represent either the numerator or the denominator. It depends on how you place the domino.

For example, this domino 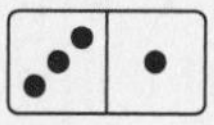 can be read as either $\frac{1}{3}$ if you place it like this 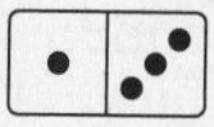 or $\frac{3}{1}$ (which is 3) if you place it like this

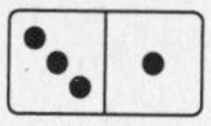

Below each equation, redraw the dominoes as necessary, write the fractions, and show the operation that makes each answer correct. The answer is always in lowest terms.

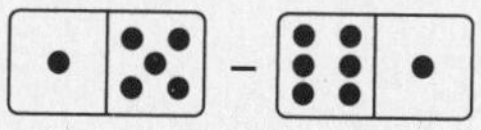

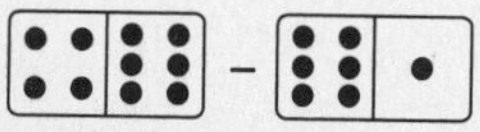

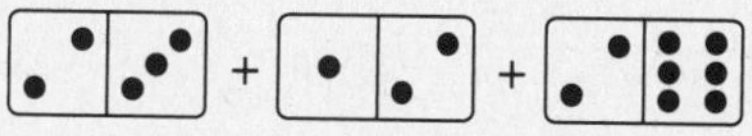

1. 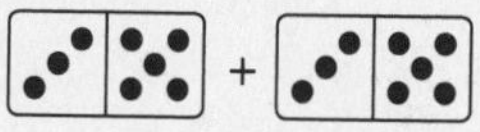 + $2\frac{4}{15}$

5. 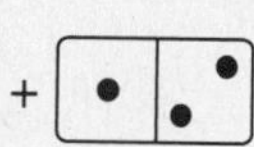 + + 3

2.  – $\frac{3}{10}$

6. 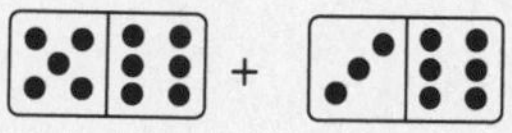 + $3\frac{1}{5}$

3. – 11

7.  – $\frac{5}{6}$

4. – $1\frac{1}{3}$

8. 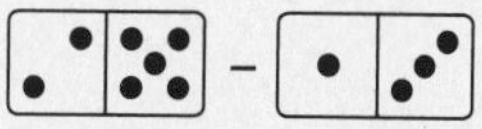 – $2\frac{1}{6}$

Name ______________________________

Advanced Domino Math

Once you understand that dominoes can represent fractions, you are ready to move to the next level of domino math.

In each problem below, redraw the dominoes as necessary, write the fractions, *and* decide whether the operation to be used should be addition or subtraction. (You will see some dominoes that you may not have seen before since the largest number of dots on half of a regular domino is 6.)

1.  $= 3\frac{1}{10}$

2.  $= 3\frac{2}{21}$

3.  $= 3\frac{7}{12}$

4. 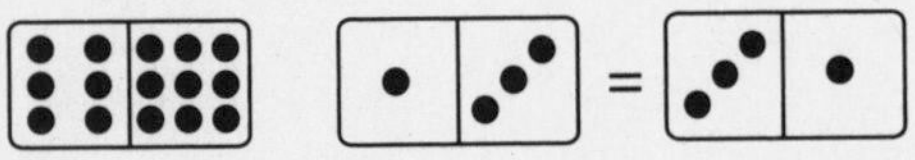 =

5. 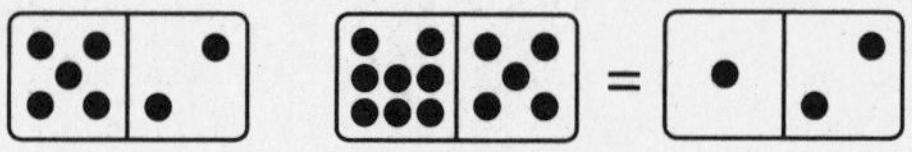 =

6.  ? $= 1\frac{1}{3}$

7. 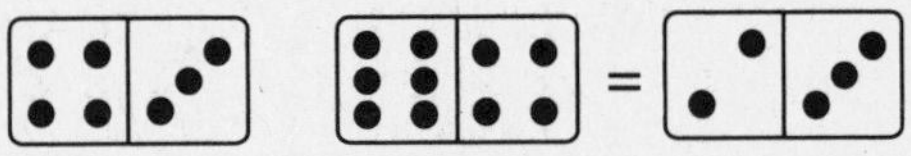  =

8.  ? $= 2\frac{3}{5}$

Name ______________________________

Concentration

Dear Family,

Your child has been measuring the length of objects in inches, feet, and yards and has also been learning how to change these measurements to smaller or larger units. You and your child can play a game to develop these skills further.

Each player measures both large and small objects around the house. After recording at least 12 measurements, players convert each to another unit. For example, 1 yd 2 in. could also be expressed as 3 ft 2 in. or as 38 in.

Next, use the measurements and their equivalencies to make a Concentration game. Each measurement is written on one index card; each equivalency is written on another. The cards are then combined, shuffled, and placed facedown on a table. Players alternate trying to turn over equivalent pairs. A player who makes a match continues his or her turn until making a mistake. The player accumulating the most pairs wins.

Name ______________________________

Sir Wexford's Quest

Help Sir Wexford find the 3 miniature knights needed to complete his collection. Counterfeits abound! The only way to identify the genuine antiques is to measure. The heights of the missing miniatures are: $1\frac{3}{8}$ in., $1\frac{3}{4}$ in., and $2\frac{1}{4}$ in. Once complete, Sir Wexford's collection will be priceless! Which of the miniature knights are the real thing?

1.

2.

3.

4.

5.

6.

Name ______________________________

Stranger than Fiction

It is often revealing to think about measurements of length in more than one way. Use the equivalencies below to solve the problems and find more facts that are stranger than fiction!

1 yd = 3 ft = 36 in. **1 mi = 1,760 yd = 5,280 ft**

1. A 21-year-old woman ate 23 frankfurters in 3 minutes 10 seconds at a 1977 contest in Philadelphia. If each frankfurter was 6 inches long, about how many yards of hot dogs did she eat? ____________

2. A giant jellyfish that washed into Massachusetts Bay had tentacles that were 120 feet long. How many yards long were the giant jellyfish's tentacles? ____________

3. In 1985 college students in Ohio made a banana split that was 4 miles long. How many feet long was the Ohio banana split? ____________

4. If a flea can easily cover $\frac{1}{3}$ yard in 1 leap, how many leaps will it take a flea to go from the head to the toes of a 6-foot-tall man? ____________

5. The tallest wedding cake ever made was a little more than 15 yards high. How many tiers did it have if each tier was about 7.5 inches high? ____________

6. In 1937 a 22-foot-long giant earthworm was found in South Africa. About how many yards long was this record-breaking earthworm? ____________

7. In 1972 a helicopter over France reached an altitude of 40,920 feet. About how many miles high was the amazingly high helicopter? ____________

Name ____

Pattern Possibilities

Quintus designs quilts. Today he is thinking about patterns based on a large square divided into 4 smaller squares. Each smaller square is then divided into 2 right triangles. He wants $\frac{1}{2}$ of the triangles to be shaded and $\frac{1}{2}$ to remain white. He has finished two possible patterns. Use the blank squares to design others.

1.

2.

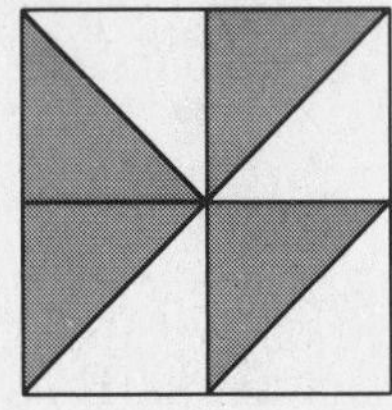

3.

4.

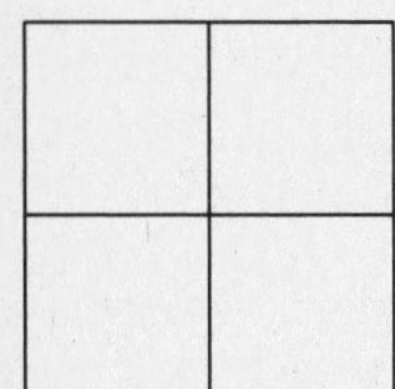

5.

6.

7.

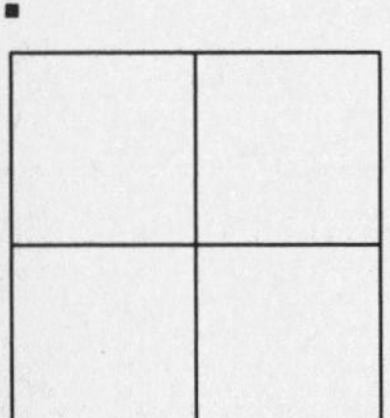

8.

9.

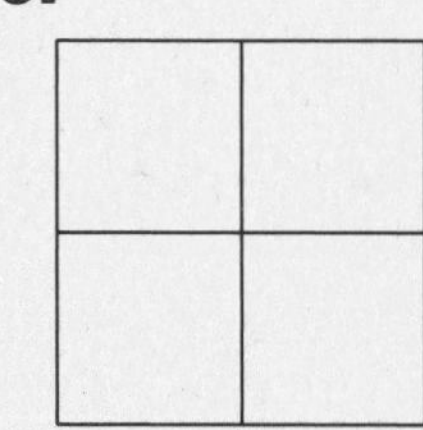

10.

11.

12.

13.

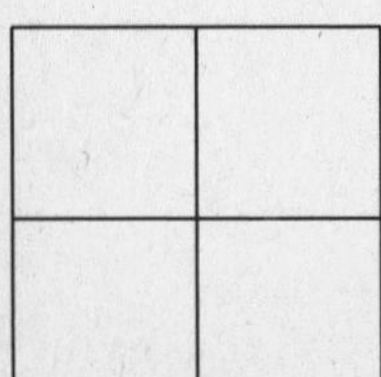

14.

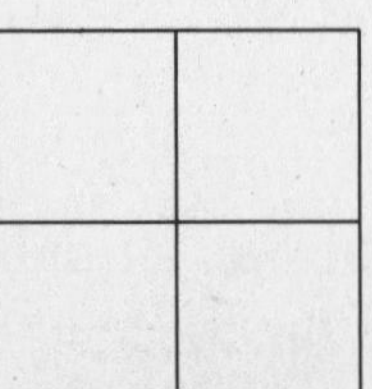

15.

Name ______________________________

Fever!

Read the graph to find out Richard's temperatures while he was sick. Then answer the questions.

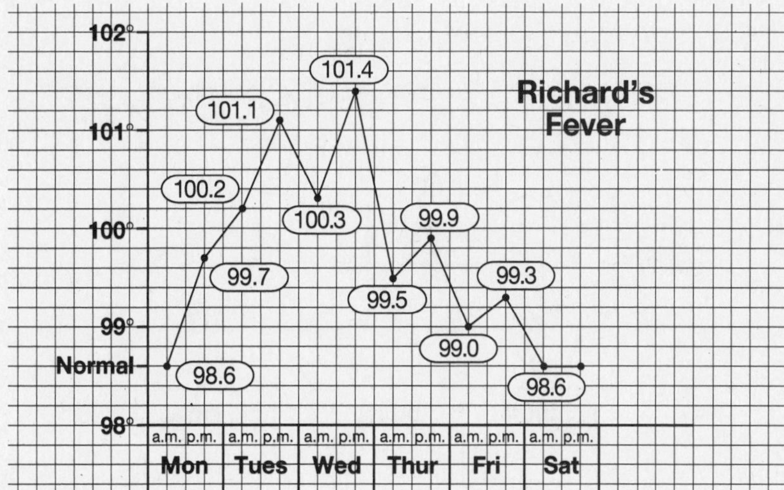

1. When was Richard's temperature first above normal? ____________

2. How far above normal did Richard's temperature rise while he was sick? ____________

3. When was Richard's temperature the highest? ____________

4. Did Richard's temperature tend to be higher each day in the morning or the afternoon? ____________

5. On which day was the greatest difference recorded between the morning and evening temperatures? ____________

6. What was the greatest recorded difference between the morning and evening temperatures of the same day? ____________

7. On what morning was there the greatest drop from the previous evening's temperature? ____________

8. How much had Richard's temperature decreased on that morning? ____________

Name ______________________________

Capacity Confusion

Louise needed a container to hold 64 fluid ounces. When she started looking for one, she realized that all her containers were labeled with different units of measurement, and none was labeled 64 oz. She made this table so she could compare her containers easily. Fill it in to see her results. Remember:

8 fl oz = 1 c	2 c = 1 pt
2 pt = 1 qt	4 qt = 1 gal

Container	ounces	cups	pints	quarts	gallons
ice cream			1		
casserole				2	
detergent	128				
bucket				10	
dutch oven		16			
paint can					1
pot				5	
milk					$\frac{1}{2}$
juice				1	
big bucket					4

Name ____________________

How Heavy Is That Hamster?

Lazy Lawrence had to know the weight of an average hamster for a science project. Unwilling to do any of his own research, he decided to ask his brother Willy the Wizard. Willy said, "I won't tell you the weight, but I will give you some easy hints so you can figure it out. Use the facts in column A to answer the multiple-choice questions in column B. If you answer them all correctly you'll have your answer at the end."

	A	B		
1.	A horse weighs about $\frac{1}{2}$ ton.	A horse weighs: 2 T	950 lb	1,000 oz
2.	One horse weighs about as much as 6 average American men.	An average man weighs: 162 lb	3,200 oz	205 lb
3.	One blue whale weighs almost as much as 2,000 men.	A blue whale weighs: 15 T	1,500 T	150 T
4.	A chimpanzee has the same weight in pounds as a blue whale has in tons.	A chimpanzee weighs: 15 lb	150 lb	1,500 lb
5.	A domestic cat weighs about $\frac{1}{10}$ what a chimpanzee weighs.	A cat weighs: 14 lb	300 oz	1.5 lb
6.	The average American woman weighs as much as $9\frac{1}{2}$ cats.	A woman weighs: 100 lb	$\frac{1}{10}$ T	135 lb
7.	It would take almost 135 rats to weigh as much as an aardvark.	A rat weighs: $\frac{1}{2}$ lb	16 oz	2 lb
8.	A hamster weighs about $\frac{1}{4}$ as much as a rat.	A hamster weighs: $\frac{1}{2}$ lb	2 lb	4 oz

Name ______________________________

Treasure Hunt Derby

Babette and Bigsby have just received their instructions for the Treasure Hunt Derby. Since both speed and accuracy are necessary for success, they have decided to estimate when they can and measure when they must. Their instructions are below. By each step write **E** if estimation is sufficient to follow the directions correctly. Write **M** if measurement is necessary.

1. Leave the start area. Ride about 4 miles north on Big Basin Road until you reach the intersection of Dry Gulch Trail. ____________

2. Travel west along Dry Gulch Trail for about 20 mi. You will come to Good Eats Grocery. ____________

3. Enter Good Eats and get the signature of a customer who is exactly 5 ft $7\frac{1}{2}$ in. tall. Be polite. ____________

4. Continue west along Dry Gulch Trail. Proceed exactly 6.8 mi past the second stoplight to the rest area at the side of the road. ____________

5. Clean the area. Put all the cans and trash you collect in one trash barrel. Place that barrel halfway between the 2 picnic tables closest to the road. ____________

6. Continue west on Dry Gulch Trail. Take the next right onto the dirt road. You will come to an empty shack on the left. In the main room there is only one floorboard with an area of exactly 240 in.^{2}. Lift this floor board. Record the time. ____________

7. Remove, but do not open, the gold velvet pouch. The pouch and its contents will be yours if you can return to the start area in no fewer than 44 and no more than 46 minutes. ____________

Name ______________________________

Playing Fields

Did you know that:

A boxing ring has an area of 37 square meters, and a Ping-Pong table has an area equal to about $\frac{1}{9}$ of that?

A soccer field has an area of 7,300 square meters, and a football field has an area equal to about $\frac{3}{4}$ of that?

A baseball diamond has an area of 754 square meters, and a tennis court has an area equal to about $\frac{1}{3}$ of that?

An ice hockey rink has an area of 1,860 square meters, and a basketball court has an area equal to about $\frac{1}{5}$ of that?

An Olympic size pool has an area of 1,050 square meters, and a water polo pool has an area equal to about $\frac{3}{5}$ of that?

A judo mat has an area of 256 square meters, and a karate mat has an area equal to exactly $\frac{1}{4}$ of that?

Use estimation to write the correct size of each playing area.

600 sq m	4.16 sq m
261 sq m	64 sq m
5,358 sq m	364 sq m

Ping-Pong table ______________ football field ______________

tennis court ______________ water polo pool ______________

basketball court ______________ karate mat ______________

Name ____________________

Athletic Equipment

To decrease its inventory, the Run Around Athletic Company put the following items on sale:

	Regular Price	Save		Regular Price	Save
Running shoes	\$49	$\frac{1}{5}$	Tennis rackets	\$74	$\frac{1}{3}$
Basketball shoes	\$59	$\frac{1}{3}$	Socks	\$ 3	$\frac{1}{4}$
Baseball cleats	\$89	$\frac{1}{10}$	Wristbands	\$ 2	$\frac{1}{2}$
Running shorts	\$27	$\frac{1}{4}$	Soccer balls	\$35	$\frac{1}{4}$
T-shirts	\$19	$\frac{1}{5}$	Barbells	\$31	$\frac{1}{2}$
Headbands	\$ 5	$\frac{1}{3}$	Gloves	\$ 9	$\frac{1}{5}$

Substitute compatible numbers to answer the questions.

1. Jason bought a pair of running shoes and a pair of running shorts. About how much did he save?

____

2. Carl bought a T-shirt and a tennis racket. Sara bought basketball shoes and 6 pairs of socks. Who saved more?

____

3. Sal bought 3 soccer balls and one set of barbells. Did he spend more or less than \$100?

____

4. Tina spent \$40. Could she have bought 5 pairs of gloves? Explain.

____

____

____

Name ______________________________

The Eating Contest

You have entered a contest to become the world's champion sandwich eater. You have already put away $\frac{1}{4}$ of your first sandwich. If you can eat $\frac{1}{2}$ of what is left, you will get to the semifinals.

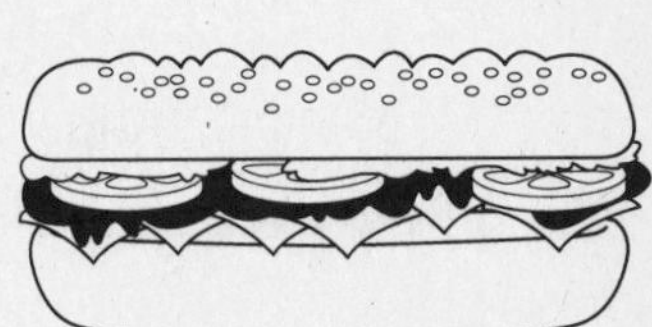

Use the picture.

Show how much you have already eaten. Cross it off.
How much is left to be eaten?

______

Divide what is left to be eaten into 3 equal parts.
What part of the whole sandwich does each part represent?

______

Divide each of the 3 parts in half. What part of the whole sandwich does each of these parts represent?

______

Write a fraction other than the one above that names the part of the sandwich left to be eaten.

______

How much must you still eat in order to get to the semifinals?

______

Complete these multiplication sentences:

$\frac{1}{2}$ of $\frac{3}{4}$ = ______ $\frac{1}{2} \times \frac{6}{8}$ = ______

How do these multiplication sentences relate to the sandwich story?

____

____

Name ____________________

Fraction Action

Dear Family,
We are studying multiplication of fractions in class. This game can help students multiply fractions and improve their number sense.

Number of Players: 2 or more

Materials: number cube or spinner marked 1–6

How to Play:

Each player copies the diagram below.

$$\frac{\square}{\square} \times \frac{\square}{\square} =$$

Take turns rolling the cube or spinning the spinner. With each roll, all players write the number rolled in any square they wish. However, once a number is placed, it may not be moved. After 4 rolls, multiply the fractions. The player with the largest product wins the round. The first player to win 3 rounds wins the game.

Variations:

Player with the smallest product wins.

Player with the product closest to 1 wins.

Player with the product closest to $\frac{1}{2}$ wins.

Change the diagram to $\square \times \frac{\square}{\square}$, to multiply a whole number by a fraction.

Name ______________________________

A Number Trick

Have you ever seen a magician perform feats of magic? Magicians are able to impress us because they know the explanation for what they are doing, and we do not. Here is a chance for you to act like a magician and impress your family or friends with a number trick (unless, of course, they have read this page!).

You say:	Why it works:
1. "Think of any number."	Let a variable, x, be the number.
2. "Now add 3 to it."	The value is now $(x + 3)$.
3. "Multiply by 2."	2 times $(x + 3)$ is $(2x + 6)$.
4. "Now subtract 4."	$(2x + 6) - 4$ is $(2x + 2)$.
5. "Divide by 2."	$(2x + 2)$ divided by 2 is $(x + 1)$.
6. "Finally, subtract the number you began with."	Remember, you began with x, so $(x + 1) - x$ always leaves 1.
7. "Your answer is 1."	The answer is always 1.

When you multiplied in step 3, you multiplied both the variable x and the number 3. In which other step did you perform an operation on both the variable and the whole number? __________

When you added a whole number in step 2, you did not do anything to the variable. In which other step did you perform an operation on a whole number but not on a variable? __________

Which is the only step in which you performed an operation on a variable but not on a whole number? __________

Name ____________________

Lionel's Burgers

Read each problem and think about how you would solve it. Then decide in which category at the bottom of the page the problem belongs.

Burger Haven			
Hamburger	$ .95	Salad	$ .60
Doubleburger	1.70	Large fries	.79
Cheeseburger	1.30	Onion rings	1.35
Double Cheeseburger	1.95	Lemonade	.45
		Large Lemonade	.70

1. Lionel spent $3.90 on cheeseburgers over 3 days. He spent the same amount each day. How much did he spend each day?

____

2. He spent $1.70 a day on double cheeseburgers for 5 days. How much did he spend?

____

3. For one lunch, he ordered a burger, salad, and a small lemonade. How much did he spend? ____________________

4. One night for dinner he had 2 double burgers, onion rings, and a large lemonade. How much did he spend?

____

5. For Saturday lunch, he ordered a burger and salad and paid with a $5 bill. How much change did he get?

____

6. Over a period of one week, these were his lunch bills: $2.30, $3.39, $3.75, and $2.40. What was his total for the week?

____

7. One day he ordered nothing but 3 orders of onion rings. Then he realized he only had $4.00. Was that enough money?

____

8. One dinner cost Lionel $2.44. What did he order?

____

Name ____

Carpeting Concerns

The Ambersons, the Andersons, the Alversons, and the Allisons are all shopping for carpeting at the We've Got You Covered Carpeting Company. Since every adult member of each family is a math teacher, they are driving the salesman crazy with their explanations of what they need. Here is what each family said, in the order they are listed above:

"When you multiply the dimensions of our room, you see that we need the most carpeting."

"Ours is the smallest room, but we're happy."

"Ours is the only room where the product of the dimensions is a whole number."

"Ours is the only room where the product of the dimensions is a mixed number already in lowest terms."

Write the name of each family and the area in square feet inside the outline of their room.

$12\frac{1}{2}$ ft

$10\frac{4}{5}$ ft

$11\frac{1}{3}$ ft

$9\frac{1}{4}$ ft

$13\frac{1}{5}$ ft

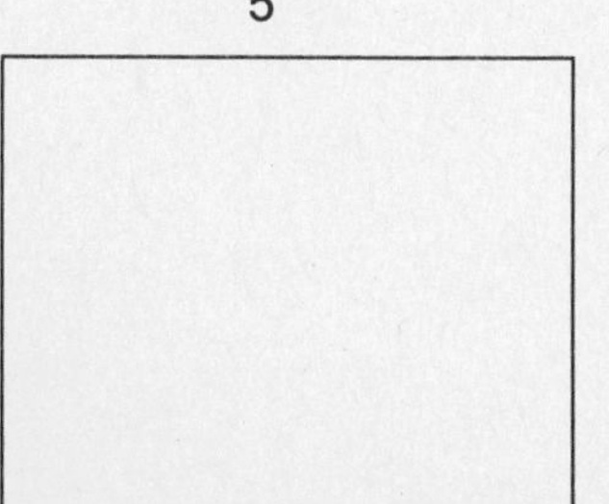

$10\frac{1}{2}$ ft

$12\frac{1}{4}$ ft

11 ft

Name ______________________________

Hidden Fractions

> Dear Family,
> Your child has been learning how to use a calculator to perform operations with the decimal equivalents of common fractions. This activity will help make clear the relationship between fractions and decimals.

Look at this equation: 1 2 3 4 = 3 8

By itself, it makes no sense. However, if you include the signs shown below, it becomes a true equation:

$1 \div 2 \times 3 \div 4 = 3 \div 8$ since $\frac{1}{2} \times \frac{3}{4} = \frac{3}{8}$

Use these equalities:

$\frac{3}{8} = 0.375$ $\frac{6}{7} = 0.857$

$\frac{2}{3} = 0.666$ $\frac{4}{9} = 0.444$

$\frac{1}{20} = 0.05$

Press the following keys on your calculator to see the equality:

[AC] [1] [÷] [2] [×] [3] [÷] [4] [=]

You can also multiply a fraction by a whole number on a calculator:

1 3 2 = 2 3 Where would you place one × sign and two ÷ signs to make a true equation?

____

Work together to make true equations. Check with a calculator and the equality table at the top of the page.

1. 1 4 1 5 = 1 2 0 with three ÷ signs and one × sign

____

2. 2 3 7 = 6 7 with two ÷ signs and one × sign

____

3. 2 9 2 = 4 9 with two ÷ signs and one × sign

____

Name ______________________________

Tangram Fractions

Trace the tangram. Cut out the seven pieces.

If the large square is 1 whole unit, what is the value of each of the other pieces?

You can use the tangram pieces to help understand dividing fractions. For example:

How many 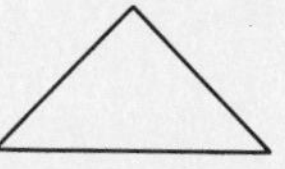 are there in 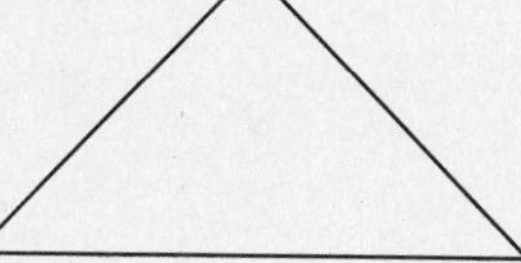

is the same as this division: $\frac{1}{4} \div \frac{1}{16} = ?$

By moving the small piece over the large one, you can see that the answer is 4. So $\frac{1}{4} \div \frac{1}{16} = 4$.

Divide. Use the tangram pieces to help you.

1. $\frac{1}{4} \div \frac{1}{8} =$ ______

2. $\frac{3}{8} \div \frac{1}{16} =$ ______

3. $\frac{1}{8} \div \frac{1}{16} =$ ______

4. $1 \div \frac{1}{4} =$ ______

5. $\frac{1}{2} \div \frac{1}{4} =$ ______

6. $\frac{2}{4} \div \frac{1}{8} =$ ______

Name ______________________________

What Is the Rule?

Each group of figures below has been separated into 2 groups according to their characteristics. Explain the characteristics used to classify each group.

1.

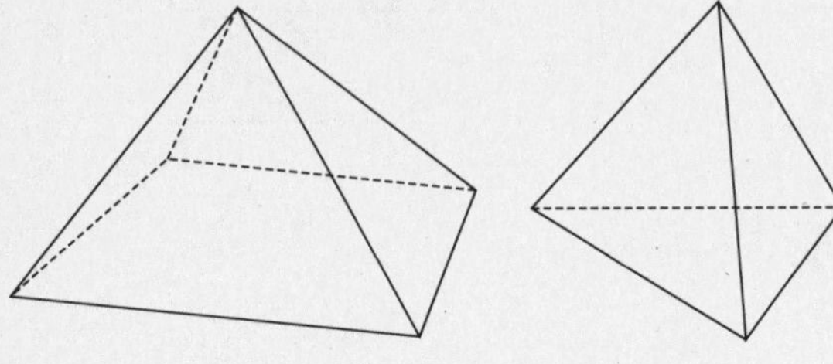

______________________ ______________________

2.

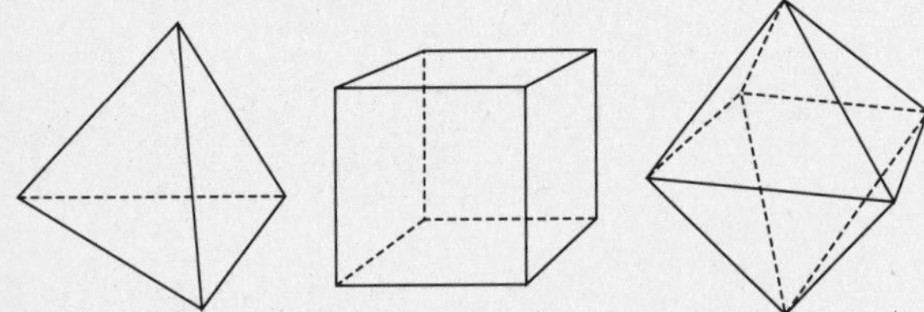

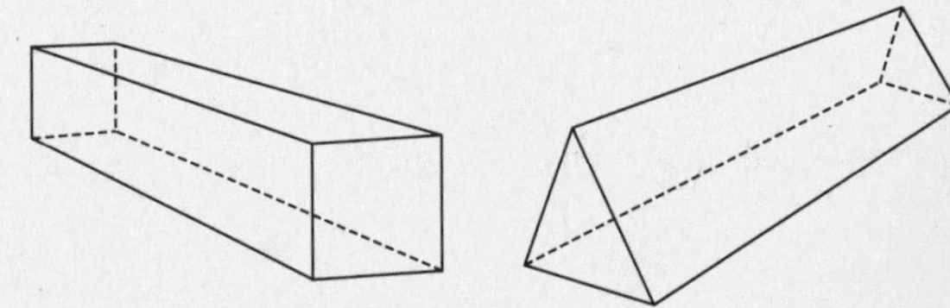

______________________ ______________________

3.

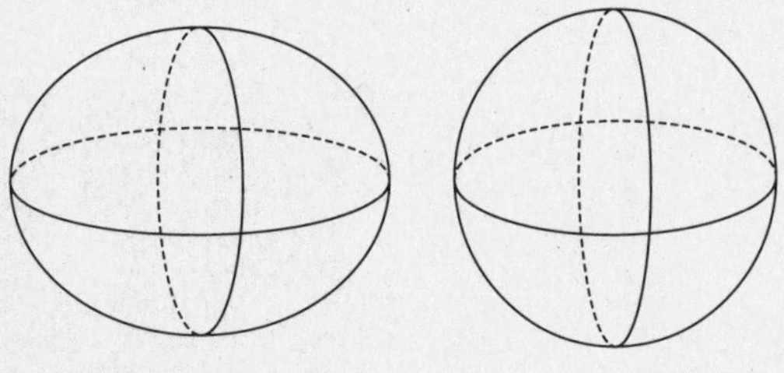

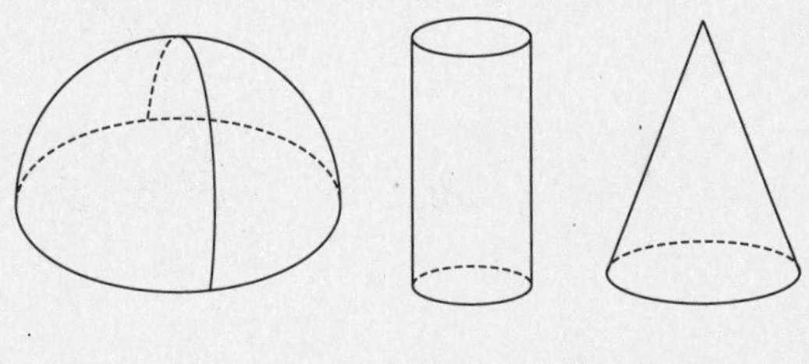

______________________ ______________________

4.

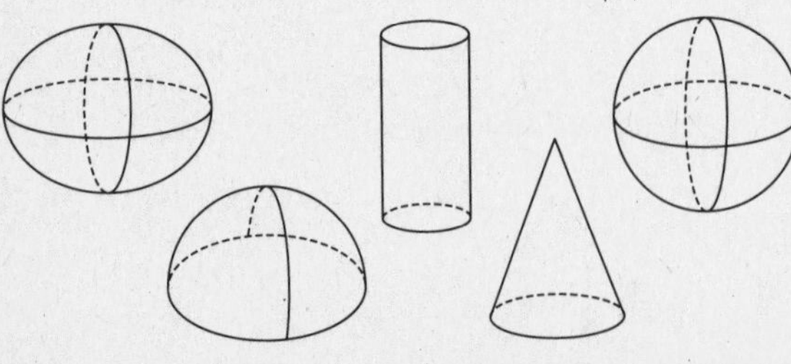

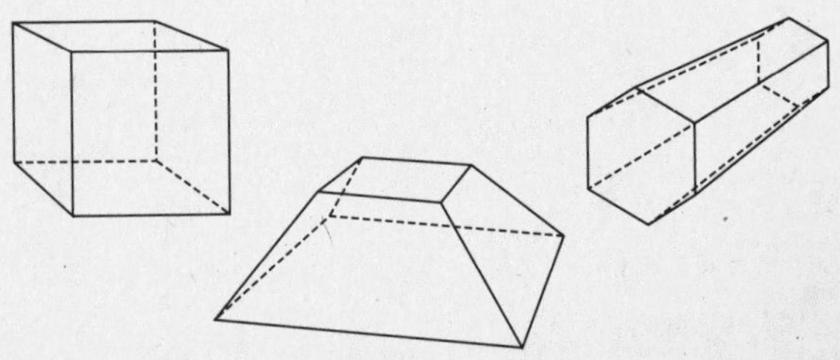

______________________ ______________________

Name ______________________________

Possible or Impossible Triangles?

Cut thin strips of paper to the needed lengths. Then answer each question for the strips you have cut.

- Is it possible to arrange the strips to form a triangle?
- If the answer is yes, what kind of triangle can you form? Sketch the triangle.

1. 3 in., 5 in., 6 in.

2. 2 in., 5 in., 8 in.

3. 3 in., 4 in., 5 in.

4. 2 in., 3 in., 6 in.

5. 2 in., 6 in., 8 in.

6. 3 in., 3 in., 4 in.

Think about what you have just done.

In order for 3 line segments to form a triangle, what must be true about their lengths?

____

____

Name ____

Angle Measures

Trace the figure below onto a sheet of paper and cut it out.

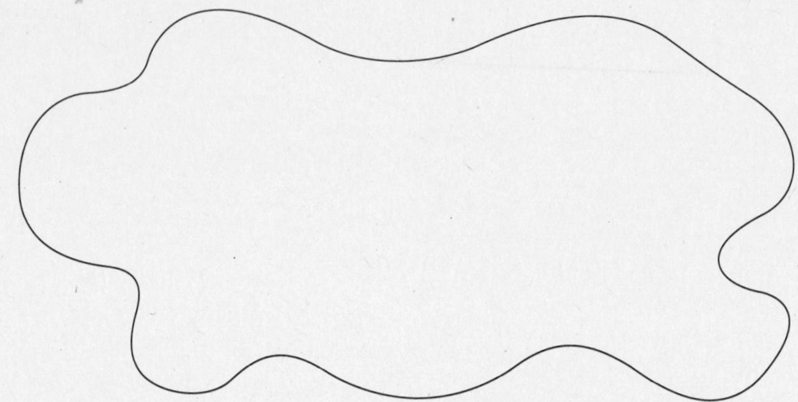

A. Without using a ruler, protractor, pencil, or any other tool, how can you create a right angle on the paper?

____

B. When you have solved Problem A, use your right angle to help you decide which of each pair of angles below is larger. Put the square corner into both angles. The one that can contain more of the square corner is larger. If they can both contain the square corner, the one that has more left over is larger. The first one is done for you.

1.

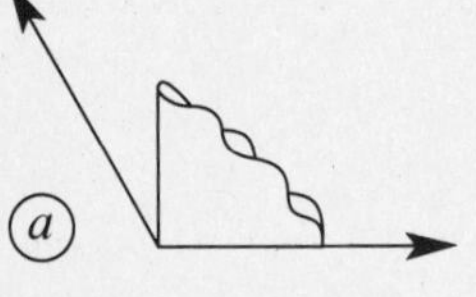

b

2.

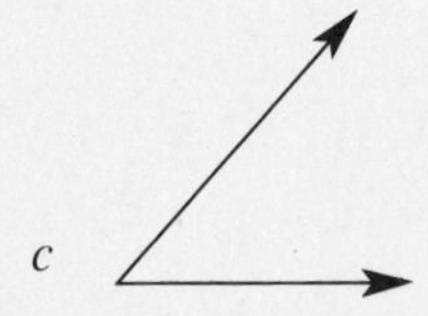

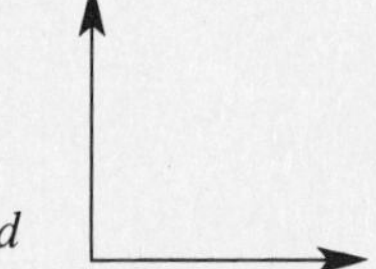

3.

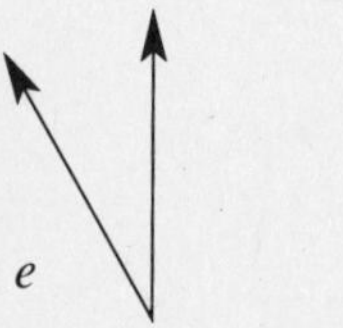

f

4.

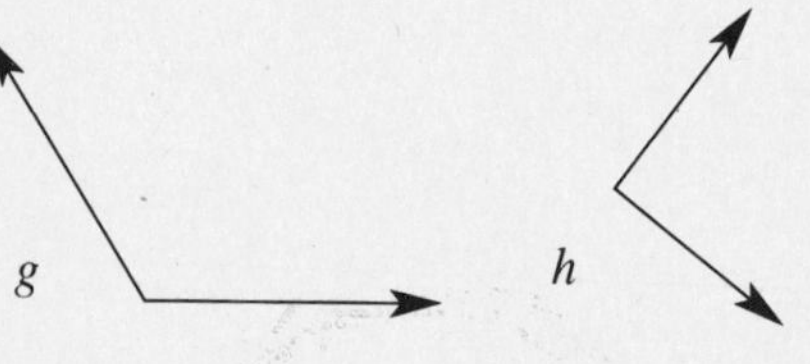

5.

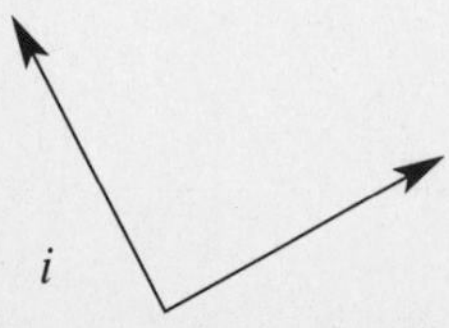

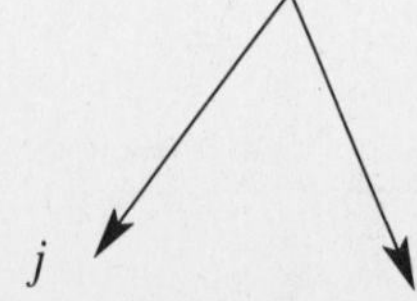

6.

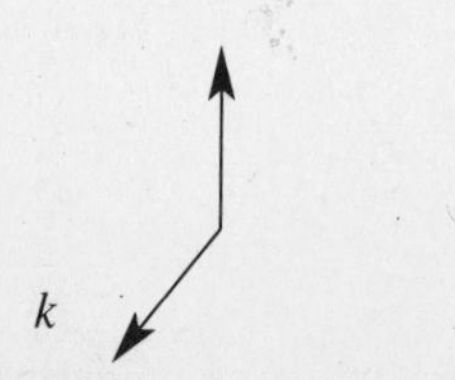

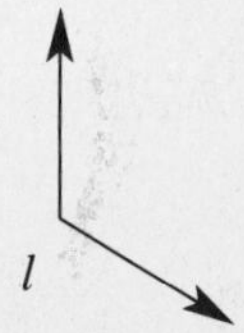

Name ______________________________

Tangrams

A tangram is an ancient puzzle that mathematicians think may have been invented in China.

Trace this tangram onto a sheet of unlined paper. Label each piece as shown. Then cut it out and cut out the 7 pieces. How would you describe the 7 pieces?

____

____

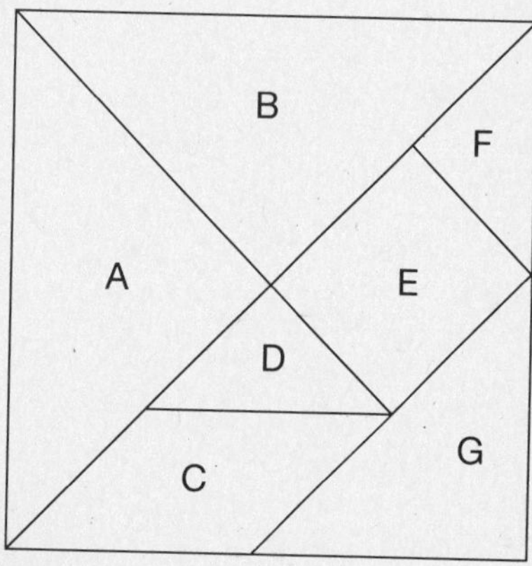

For each exercise below, use the pieces to make the quadrilateral. Then sketch the figure.

1. Square using D, F, G

2. Rectangle using C, D, E, F

3. Rhombus using D, F

4. Parallelogram using A, D, F, G

5. Trapezoid using D, E, F

6. Square using A, D, F, G

Name ____

All in the Family

The drawing shows the relationship between members of the quadrilateral "family." Notice that each "flow chart" shape reflects its name. Each arrow points to the next most general quadrilateral. The drawing shows, for example, that every rectangle is also a parallelogram.

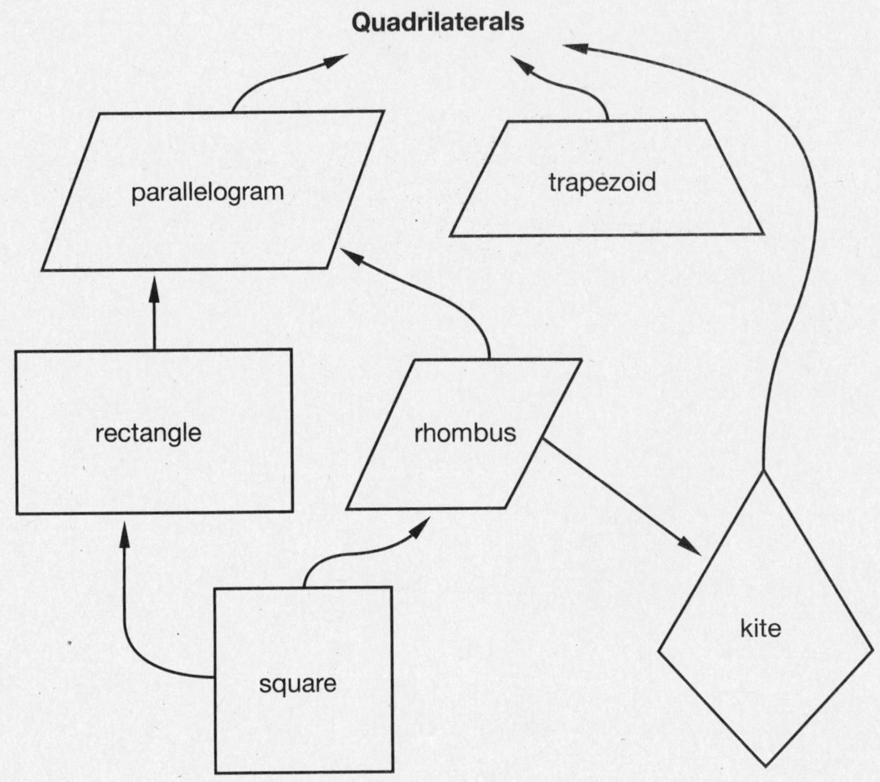

Use the drawing to write **true** or **false** for each statement.

1. Every rhombus is also a parallelogram. ______________

2. Every square is also a rhombus and a kite. ______________

3. Every trapezoid is also a quadrilateral. ______________

4. Every rhombus is also a square. ______________

5. Every kite is also a rhombus and a square. ______________

6. Every parallelogram is also a rectangle. ______________

Name ______________________________

The Envelope, Please

Here is another experiment to support Mr. Lively's conclusion. Follow these steps:

1. On a sheet of unlined paper draw *any* triangle and cut it out.

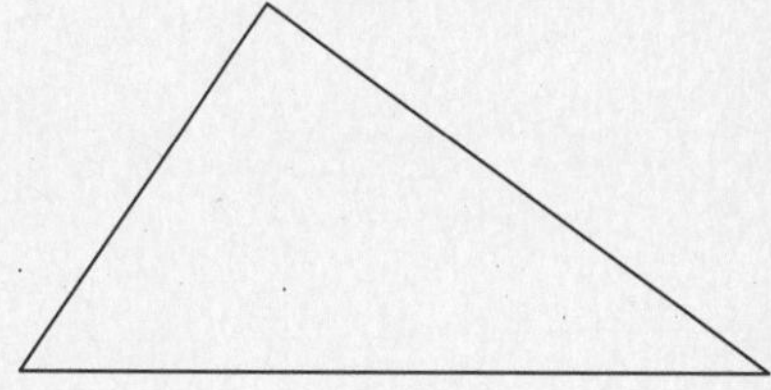

2. Fold both of the two shorter sides over onto themselves to find their midpoints. Connect the midpoints to each other with a line segment.

3. Draw straight lines from the midpoints to the third side so that they form right angles with the third side.

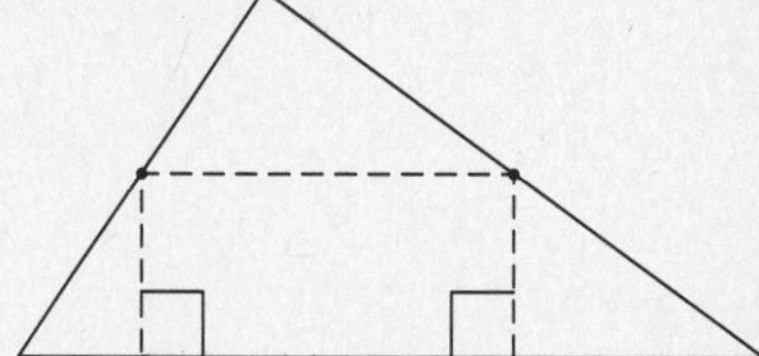

4. Fold the 3 small triangles over the 3 lines like an envelope.

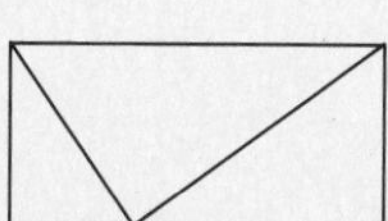

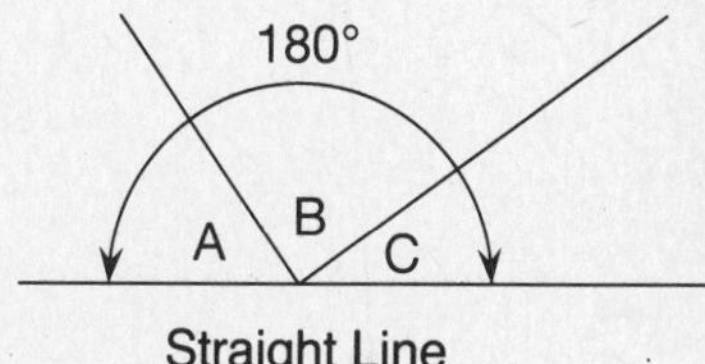

Straight Line

Do you see that the 3 angles meet at a point and exactly form a straight line?

How does this experiment help to support Mr. Lively's conclusion?

____

____

____

Name ______________________________

Flip Images

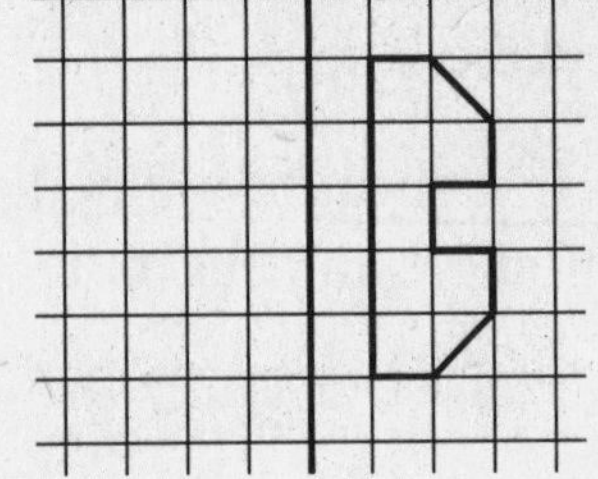

Use centimeter graph paper.

Draw a heavy solid line down the center of the paper.

Copy the picture shown at the right. Then fold the paper over the center line.

Press down hard on each vertex of the figure so you leave a mark on the other side when you unfold the paper. If you cannot press hard enough, use a pin to push through each vertex.

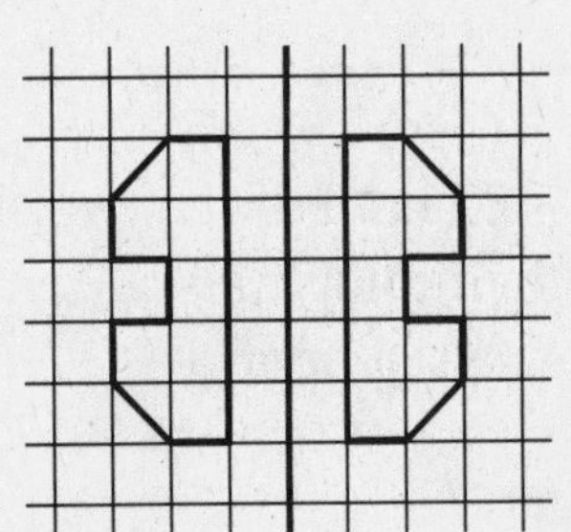

Now unfold the paper and connect vertices of the new figure. This is the **flip image** of the original figure. The heavy line you drew is called the **flip line** or the line of symmetry.

1. Are the two figures congruent? How do you know?

____

2. Mark a point, call it *P*, anywhere on the original figure. Mark the same point, call it *S*, on the flip image. Connect *P* to *S* with a line segment. What is true about the distances of *P* and *S* from the flip line?

____

3. What kind of angle does line segment *PS* make with the flip line?

____

4. Try several other pairs of points. Are they always the same distance from the flip line?

____

5. When you connect other pairs of points, do they always form a right angle with the flip line?

____

Name ____________________

Animal Estimates

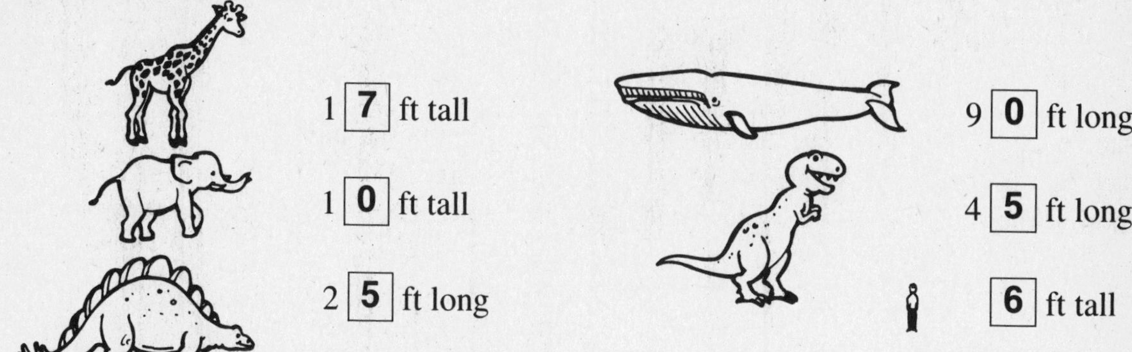

Estimate answers to the questions using the data in the picture. Then use an encyclopedia to check whether your answers are reasonable. Heights and lengths are averages.

1. If a giraffe stood on an elephant's back, what height could it reach? ____________________

2. If a stegosaurus and a blue whale stood end to end, would they be more than 130 ft long? ____________________

3. If 5 tyrannosauruses stood behind one another in a line, would the line be more than 200 ft long? ____________________

4. Would 4 men standing on one another's shoulders equal the height of one giraffe? ____________________

5. What is the fewest number of stegosauruses you would need to stand end to end to be certain of equaling the length of one blue whale?

____

6. If a blue whale, a tyrannosaurus, and a stegosaurus stood end to end, what length would they be? ____________________

Name ______________________________

Tessellations

You have seen that some regular polygons will tessellate. You can experiment to find other figures that will also tessellate.

Trace each of the figures below. Then slide the tracing paper and trace the figure again. Make at least 10 tracings before you decide whether the figure will tessellate. Write **yes** or **no** for each.

1.

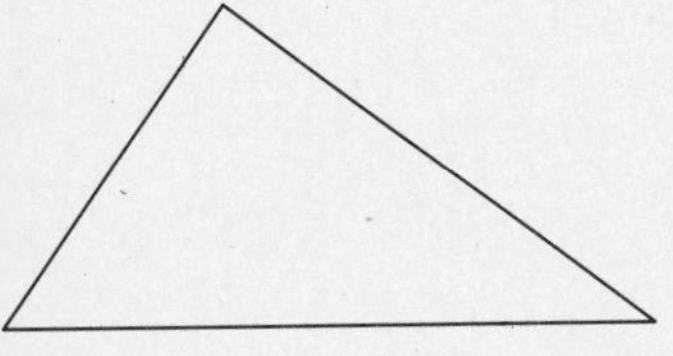

____

2.

____

3.

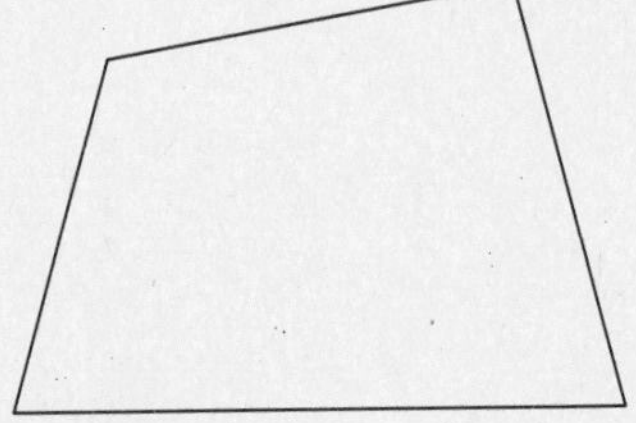

____

4.

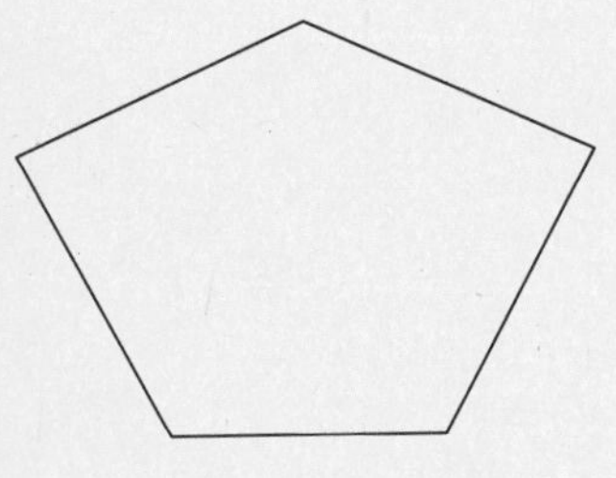

____

5.

____

6.

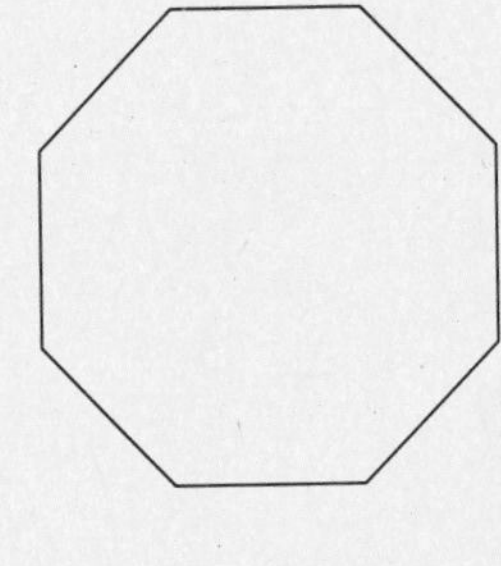

____

Look at one vertex of each figure that tessellates. What do you think must happen at each vertex if a figure is to tessellate?

____

____

____

Name ______________________________

Circle Designs

Many interesting designs can be made using only a compass, straightedge (it does not have to be a ruler), and a pencil.

The design on this page was made in 4 steps. Look at each picture, then write what was done at that step. When you finish, you may want to make a larger copy and color it in an interesting way. You can also create your own designs.

1.

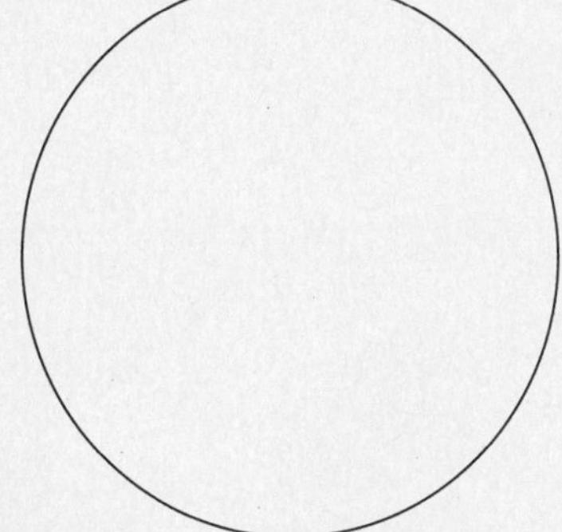

____

____

____

2.

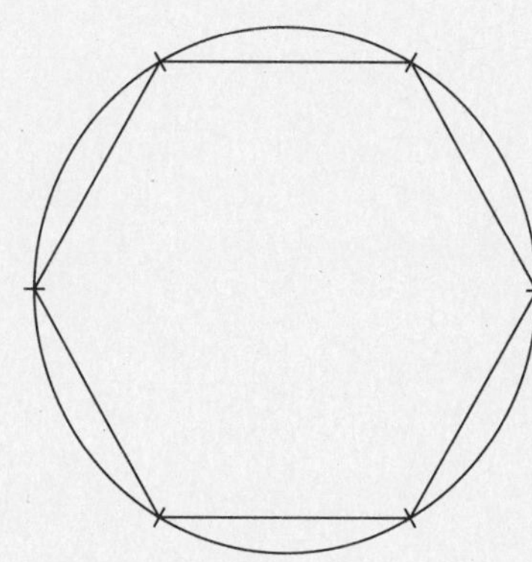

____

____

____

3.

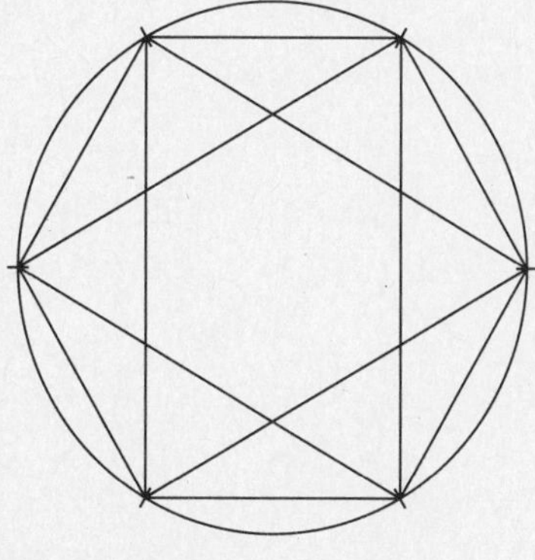

____

____

____

4.

____

____

____

Name ______________________________

Buried Treasure

Pirate Pete and his pet parrot Percy (try saying *that* three times!) found this treasure map leading to a pot of gold. Being luckier than most people, Pete noticed that the map also had instructions. They read:

> Start at the center. Each step will tell you first the circle to move to, then the number of degrees to move around the circumference of that circle. Move right along the horizontal line first. Always move around each circle in a counterclockwise direction. Always begin each step from where you finished the last one. Always take the shortest possible route between circles.

Treasure Map

The map listed these 8 steps:

1. C 45 °

2. D 90°

3. E 135°

4. A 45°

5. B 180°

6. D 0°

7. D 90°

8. E 135°

After the first two steps, Pete and Percy were at the spot marked X. Do you see why?

____

____

Can you help them locate the buried treasure?

____

Name ______________________________

Slide Images

You can draw congruent figures on centimeter graph paper using slides.

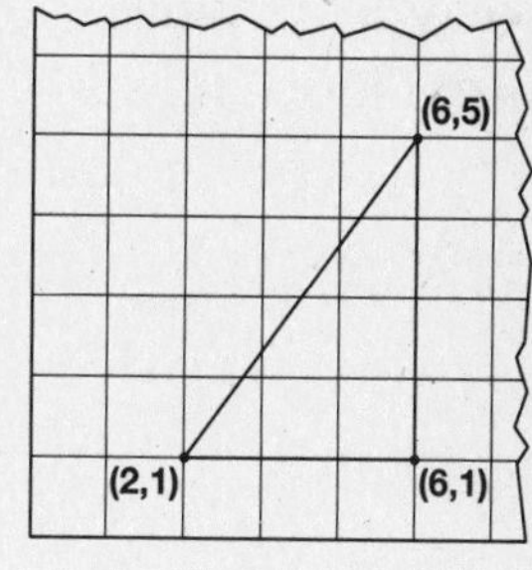

Draw the triangle at the right and label the vertices. Use the left and bottom lines as the axes.

Draw a triangle congruent to this one by using a slide. Follow these steps:

- Trace the triangle onto a sheet of tracing paper.
- Slide the tracing paper 4 cm horizontally. Push down hard on the vertices of the triangle so you leave a mark on the graph paper.
- Remove the tracing paper and connect the vertices of the new triangle.
- Can you name the vertices of the new triangle?

  ____

The new triangle is called a **slide image** of the original and is congruent to the original.

The slide you drew could be described by this symbol: ⟶

The arrow shows both the direction and length of the slide. How long is the arrow? __________

On the same sheet of graph paper, draw a slide image of the original triangle using this symbol as your guide:

- What direction will the slide be?

  ____

- How long will the slide be? __________
- What points name the vertices of the new triangle?

  ____

Name ______________________________

Club Count

Hillview School has an Art Club and a Science Club for fifth- and sixth-grade students. Each club has fewer than 30 members. Use the information below to complete each chart.

Art Club		
Interest	5th Grade	6th Grade
Pencil Sketching		
Painting		4
Pottery		
Metal Sculpture		
Total		

Science Club		
Interest	5th Grade	6th Grade
Space		
Rocks & Minerals		
Animals		
Chemistry		
Total		

1. $\frac{9}{19}$ of the students in the Art Club are fifth graders.

2. The ratio of painters to potters is 7 to 5.

3. The ratio of fifth- to sixth-grade sketchers is 3 to 2.

4. The ratio of fifth-grade potters to sixth-grade painters is 2:4.

5. 3 out of the 8 students interested in animals are fifth graders.

6. The ratio of sixth-grade space enthusiasts and rock hounds to sixth graders interested in chemistry is 5 to 6.

7. $\frac{3}{7}$ of the rock hounds are sixth graders.

8. The ratio of fifth graders interested in chemistry to all fifth-grade Science Club members is 3:12.

Name ______________________________

Super Sale Shopping

Imagine you are shopping at the Super Sale. Make ratio tables to help you solve these problems.

4 Posters for $7

SUPER SALE

Braclets 7 for $5

Glitter pens 2 for $3

Stickers 3 for 25¢

5 books for $2

1. You have $20. Could you buy 12 posters? ______________

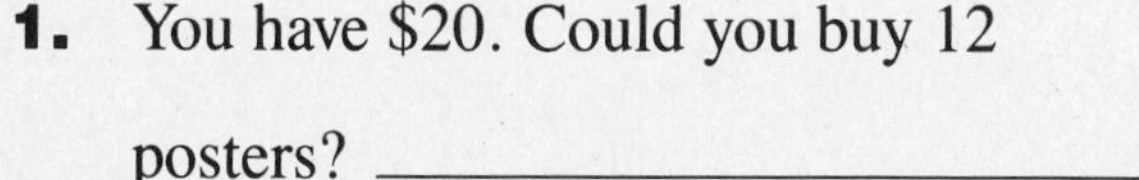

Posters	4		
Cost	$7		

2. You have $16. Could you buy 36 books? ______________

Books	5							
Cost	$2							

3. You have $10. What is the greatest number of glitter pens you could buy?

6

Pens	2			
Cost	$3			

4. You have $1.80. What is the greatest number of stickers you could buy?

21

Stickers	3						
Cost	25¢						

5. You have $15. Name the items and the amount of each you would buy.

____

____

How much money will you have left? ______________

Name ______________________________

It's in the Bag!

Work with a partner. Have your partner place 20 cubes or counters of two different colors in a bag and shake. Call one color Color A. Your job is to determine how many Color A objects are in the bag before actually looking in the bag. Here is how you can do it.

Pull	Color A Objects
1	
2	
3	
4	
5	

1. Reach into the bag and pull out 5 objects. Record how many Color A objects you pulled out in the first row of this table.

2. Put the objects back in the bag, shake, and pull out 5 again. Record the results in the second row of the table.

3. Repeat 3 more times. Be sure that you call the same color Color A each time.

4. Find the average number of Color A objects you pulled out of the bag each time.

____

5. Write a ratio comparing the average number of Color A objects to the total number of objects you pulled out of the bag each time.

____

6. Use the ratio you wrote in Step 5 to predict the total number of Color A objects in the bag.

____

7. Look in the bag. How close did you come to determining the correct number of Color A objects?

____

8. Now it's your partner's turn. Put a different combination of two colors of objects in the bag. Have your partner determine how many are Color A.

Name ______________________________

Directions . . . to Where?

Kim and Kyle found this old map and directions in the attic. They believe the Big Oak Tree is the large old tree at the back of their property. Follow the directions and draw the route on the map. Include distances in centimeters.

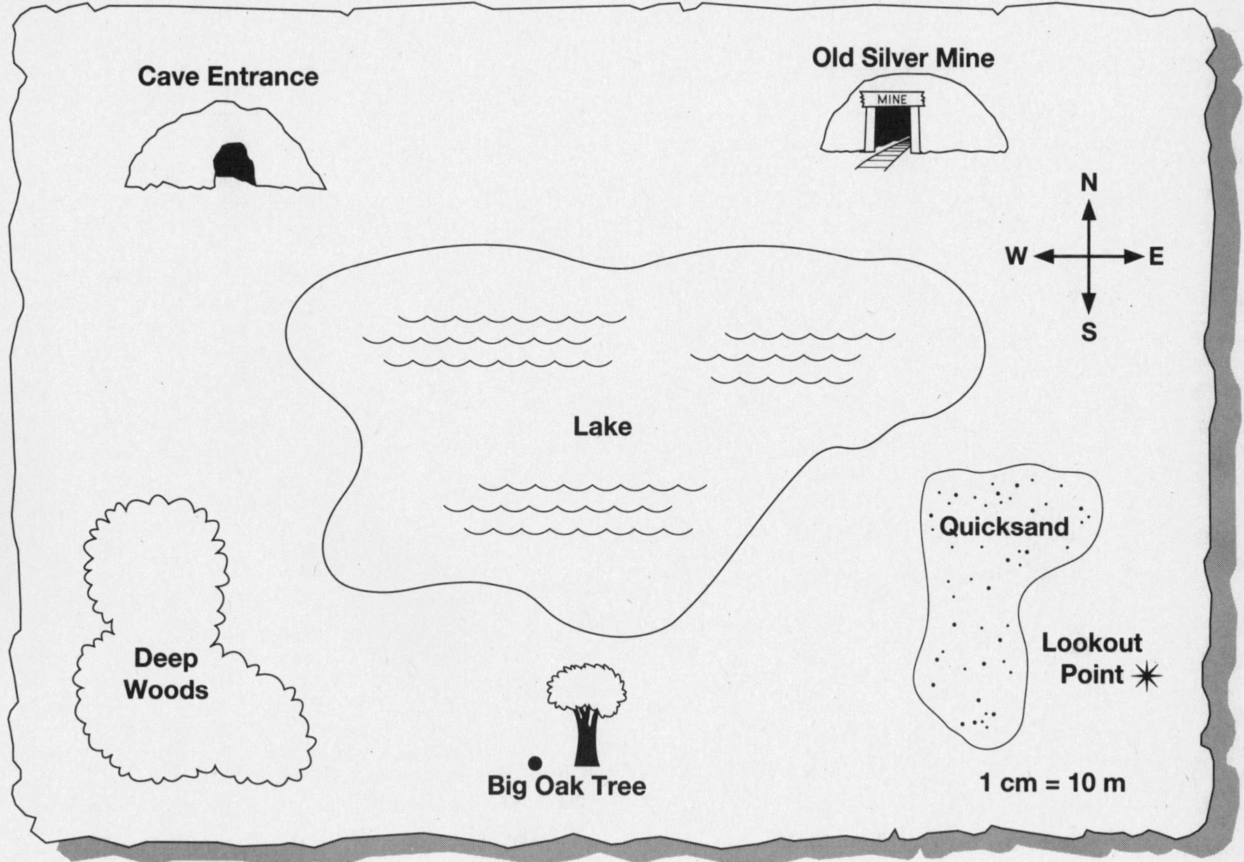

North from the Big Oak Tree	16 m
West	35 m
North	30 m
West	4 m
North	26 m
East	89 m
North	7 m

1. If Kim and Kyle follow the directions correctly, where should they get to?

____

2. Is there a shorter route Kim and Kyle could take from the Big Oak Tree to the same place? If so, write directions for that route.

____

____

Name ___________________________

Square Away with Percents

1. Make a square by shading 49% of the squares in this grid.

2. Make a square by shading 64% of the squares in this grid.

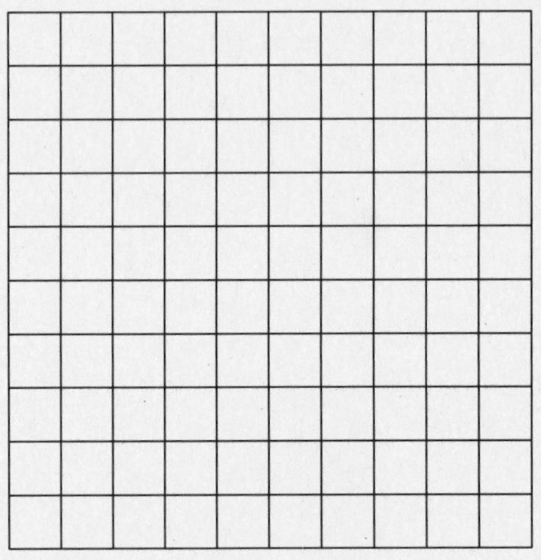

3. Name the other percents of a 10-by-10 grid you could shade to make other size squares.

____

4. Make two different size squares by shading 34% of the squares in this grid.

5. Make three different size squares by shading 56% of the squares in this grid.

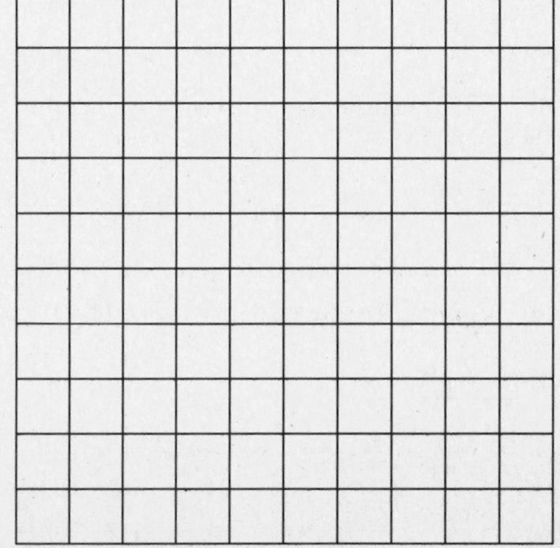

Name ______________________________

Name That Number

1. Write a percent that is greater than $\frac{91}{100}$. Its 2 digits are consecutive. ________

2. Write a 2-place decimal that is less than 40%. Its one nonzero digit is the same as the number of the grade you are in. ________

3. Write a whole-number percent that is less than 0.4. The sum of its digits is 12. ________

4. Write a percent that is greater than 0.75. One of its digits is twice its other digit. ________

5. Write a 2-place decimal that is greater than 80%. Both of its nonzero digits are different even numbers greater than 5. ________

6. Write a 2-place decimal that is less than 15%. One of its digits is the greatest 1-digit odd number. ________

7. Write a percent that is greater than $\frac{25}{100}$. The sum of its digits is 1. ________

8. Write a 2-place decimal that is greater than 39%. Its tenths digit is half its hundredths digit. ________

9. Write a 2-place decimal that is less than 30%. Each of its digits apears in 30% at least once. ________

10. Write a percent that is less than $\frac{20}{100}$. Its digit is the largest 1-digit even number. ________

Name ______________________________

Movie Mania

In a survey, teens were asked to name their favorite type of movie. The table at the right shows what percent of those surveyed preferred each type of movie. Use the information in the table to decide whether each statement is true or false. If the statement is false, tell why.

Teen Movie Preferences	
Action	25%
Comedy	24%
Horror	20%
Romance	16%
Science Fiction	15%

1. $\frac{1}{3}$ of those surveyed preferred action movies.

____

2. Only $\frac{4}{25}$ of those surveyed preferred romance movies.

____

3. $\frac{2}{5}$ of those surveyed preferred either comedy or romance movies.

____

4. $\frac{1}{4}$ more of those surveyed preferred action movies than preferred science fiction movies.

____

____

5. Over $\frac{1}{2}$ of those surveyed preferred action, horror, or science fiction movies.

____

Name ______________________________

Percent and Measurement

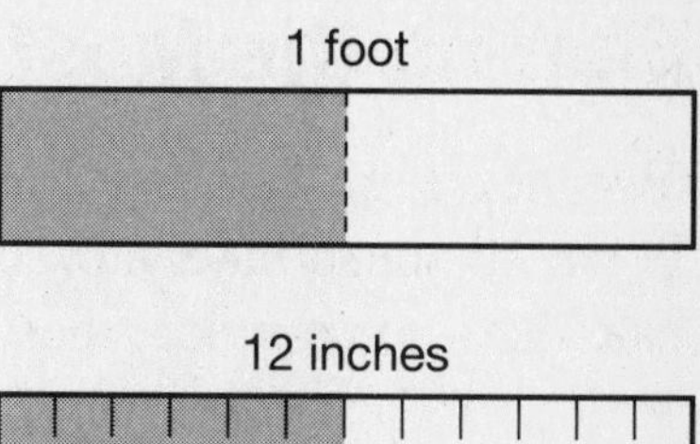

How much is 50% of 1 foot? You could answer "$\frac{1}{2}$ foot," since 50% equals $\frac{1}{2}$. Or you could answer "6 inches," since 1 foot equals 12 inches. 50%, or $\frac{1}{2}$, of 12 is 6. Use this thinking to complete each statement. Use mental math whenever you can.

1. $33\frac{1}{3}$% of 1 yd = ________ ft

2. 20% of 1 T = ________ lb

3. 75% of 1 lb = ________ oz

4. 25% of 1 yd = ________ in.

5. 50% of 1 qt = ________ pt

6. 10% of 1 T = ________ lb

These are a little harder. You may need pencil and paper.

7. 25% of 2 lb = ________ oz

8. $33\frac{1}{3}$% of 3 gal = ________ qt

9. 10% of 5 qt = ________ pt

10. 75% of 2 ft = ________ in.

11. 20% of 10 yd = ________ ft

12. 50% of 3 T = ________ lb

These are the hardest.

13. 10% of 3 ft 4 in. = ________ in.

14. 75% of 6 yd 2 ft = ________ ft

1 yd = 36 in.	1 T = 2,000 lb	1 gal = 4 qt
1 yd = 3 ft	1 lb = 16 oz	1 qt = 2 pt
1 ft = 12 in.		

Name ______________________________

Getting the Most for Your Money

Two stores are having a sale on bicycles. Imagine that you want to buy a 10-speed bike, a cycling helmet, and a water bottle. Use your calculator to complete these charts. Then answer the questions.

The Bicycle Shop				
Item	Regular Price	Sale	Save	Sale Price
10-speed bike	$180	25% off	$45	$135
cycling helmet	$20	20% off		
water bottle	$5	50% off		

Bike Bonanza				
Item	Regular Price	Sale	Save	Sale Price
10-speed bike	$160	15% off		
cycling helmet	$18	10% off		
water bottle	$6	25% off		

1. If you shopped before the sale, where would you have bought each item? Why?

____

____

____

2. If you shopped during the sale, where would you have bought each item? Why?

____

____

____

3. What else would you consider besides price when deciding where to buy your bike, helmet, and water bottle?

____

____

Name ______________________________

Amusing Problems

Choose a strategy from the Strategy List below to solve each problem. Write the strategy you chose. Then write another problem about World of Fun that uses the same strategy.

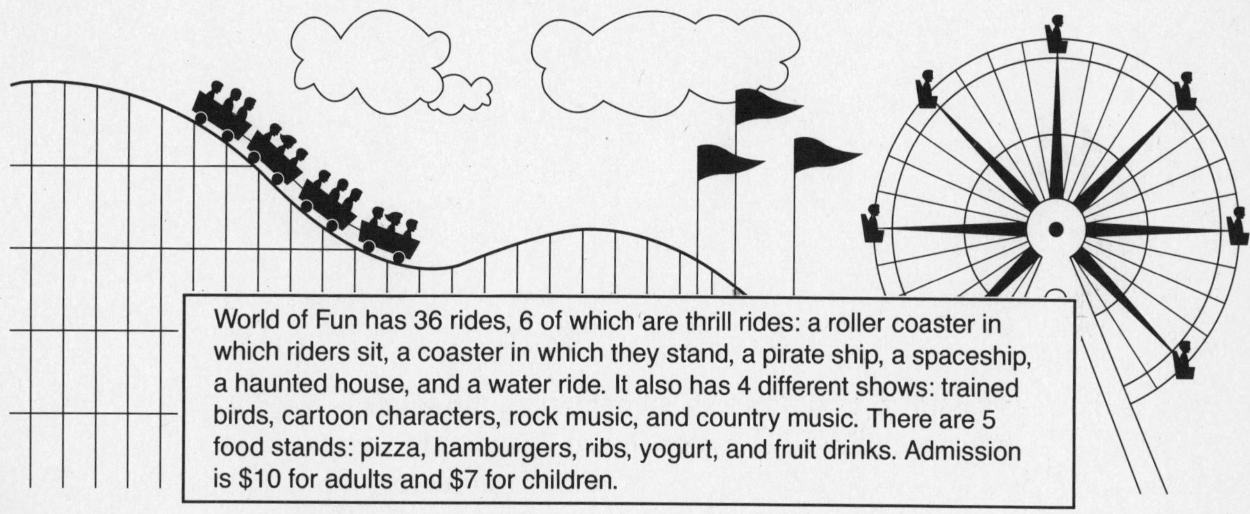

World of Fun has 36 rides, 6 of which are thrill rides: a roller coaster in which riders sit, a coaster in which they stand, a pirate ship, a spaceship, a haunted house, and a water ride. It also has 4 different shows: trained birds, cartoon characters, rock music, and country music. There are 5 food stands: pizza, hamburgers, ribs, yogurt, and fruit drinks. Admission is $10 for adults and $7 for children.

1. Before the Ortegas left World of Fun, they decided to ride on one more thrill ride and then go to one more show. How many different ways could they have done this?

____

2. Your problem: ______________________________

____

____

____

3. While at World of Fun, the Nelsons rode 75% of the rides. How many different rides did they go on?

____

4. Your problem: ______________________________

____

____

____

Problem Solving Strategies List

Act Out	Draw a Picture	Solve a Simpler Problem	Work Backwards
Use Objects	Guess and Check	Make an Organized List	Look for a Pattern
Choose an Operation	Make a Table		Use Logical Reasoning

Name ______________________________

Odd and Even Subtraction

Play this game with a friend. One player is Odd, the other player is Even. You will need 2 number cubes or spinners—one shows the numbers 13-18, the other shows the numbers 2-7.

Rules:

Players take turns tossing the number cubes or spinning the spinners and finding the difference of the 2 numbers shown. If the difference is odd, Odd scores 1 point. If the difference is even, Even scores 1 point. After 50 rounds, the player with the most points wins.

Next, complete the table below to show all the possible outcomes of each toss or spin.

–	13	14	15	16	17	18
2		12		14		16
3	10		12		14	
4		10		12		14
5	8		10		12	
6		8		10		12
7	6		8		10	

Now circle all the possible odd outcomes on the table. Notice how this compares with the possible number of even outcomes. Is the game fair or unfair? Explain.

____

____

____

Name ______________________________

A Fair Choice?

Mr. Webster must choose one member of his drama club to help perform magic tricks at the next assembly. He decided to draw a name from a box, but Shelley cried out that this was not fair. Was it fair?

To investigate, take 6 pieces of paper of equal size. Write a different name on each piece. Then place the names in a box and draw 54 times, replacing the drawn name each time. Use the chart below to tally your results.

Name	Tally

Examine your results. Was each name equally likely to be drawn? Was each name drawn nearly the same number of times? Was the drawing fair? Explain.

____

____

____

Name ______________________________

What Are the Chances?

Study each situation. Then answer the questions.

September

Sun	Mon	Tues	Wed	Thurs	Fri	Sat
	1	2	3	4	5	6

If you asked a friend to choose a date for next week's bake sale by drawing the dates out of a hat, what are the chances your friend would choose:

1. a Friday? ______

2. a weekend date? ______

3. a Tuesday? ______

4. an even-numbered date? ______

5. an odd-numbered date? ______

6. the 12th? ______

1	2	3	4	5	6	7	8	9	10

If you mix up the numbers and choose one without looking, what are the chances of drawing:

7. a 3? ______

8. a 6 or 7? ______

9. an even number? ______

10. an odd number? ______

11. a 1? ______

12. a number less than 5? ______

13. a 2-digit number? ______

14. a 2, 4, or 6? ______

Name ______________________________

A Class Experiment

A number cube with sides 1 to 6 is tossed.
What is the mathematical probability of a rolling a 3?

______

In 60 tosses how many 3s would you expect to roll? ______

To compare the mathematical probability with the experimental probability, divide your class into 10 teams. Each team will toss the number cube 60 times and record their results. To examine all the results, use the chart below.

Team	No. of 1s	No. of 2s	No. of 3s	No. of 4s	No. of 5s	No. of 6s
A						
B						
C						
D						
E						
F						
G						
H						
I						
J						

Discuss how the mathematical probability of rolling a 3 compares with each team's experimental probability of rolling a 3.

Name ________________________________

And the Winner Is . . .

Evaluate the performance records of the runners qualified for the 100-yard dash championship. Then answer the questions.

Runner	Fastest Time	Slowest Time	Wins This Season	Total Runs for Season
Darcy	14.20	14.53	7	7
Sue	14.33	15.03	6	9
Lea	15.00	15.41	4	10
Amy	14.23	15.01	8	10
Beth	15.21	15.51	2	9
Tara	15.02	15.51	4	8

1. Is each girl equally or unequally likely to win? ____________

2. Which girl won 50% of her races? 100%? ____________

3. Predict a winner for the following pairs competing in the semifinals:

Darcy versus Sue ________ Lea versus Beth ________

Amy versus Tara ________

4. Predict a winner if the two finalists competing are Amy and Sue. Explain the reasons for your choice.

____

____

____

____

____

____

Use with text page 418.

Name ______________________________

Pizza Party

Susan needs to order pizza for 20 guests coming to her pizza party.

Peter's Pizza Palace				
Size		**Price**	**Quantity**	**Price**
Large Round	10″ diameter	8.95		
Medium Sheet	18″ × 24″	10.25		
Large Sheet	20″ × 36″	14.00		
Toppings: $0.45 extra per topping Onions, Pepperoni, Olives			Subtotal	
			7% tax	
			Total	

Solve the problems using the data from the order form.

1. Use mental math to estimate: Is the large sheet pizza about twice the size of the medium sheet pizza? ______________

2. Exactly how much larger is it? ______________

3. Susan wants to serve 4″ × 6″ pieces of pizza. Draw a diagram to help you decide how many pieces she can cut from one large sheet pizza. ______________

4. Susan orders two large sheet pizzas with pepperoni and one medium sheet pizza (plain). Estimate how much change she should get from fifty dollars. ______________

5. Find the total bill, including tax. ______________

6. Find Susan's exact change. ______________

Name ______________________________

Taking a Sample

Estimate the number of students with the given eye color in your school by using your class as a random sample. Record your data on a table or chart.

Eye Color	No. of Students
Blue	
Brown	
Other	
Total	

Answer the questions, using the data you collected.

1. For your room, find the probability of having:

blue eyes ______ brown eyes ______ other eyes ______

2. Find out the total number of students in your school. Based on your sample, what is the number you would estimate to have:

blue eyes ______ brown eyes ______ other eyes ______

3. Algebra: Let c stand for the eye color recorded most in your sample. Let m and n stand for the other colors. For the whole school, would you expect the following to be true or false? Explain. $P(c) > P(m) + P(n)$

____

Name ______________________________

Guess What?

Can you guess which symbol your partner is thinking of?

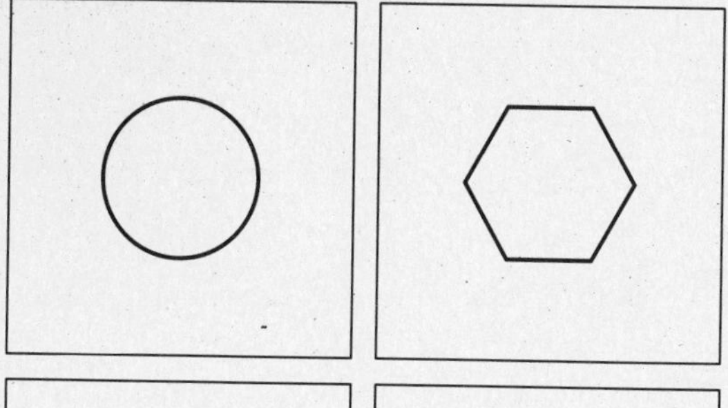

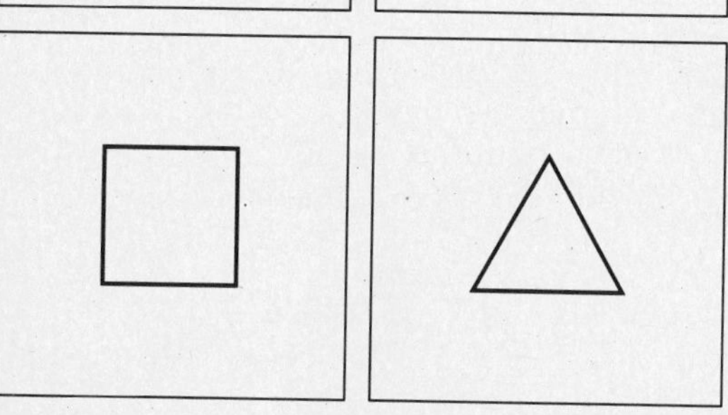

	Symbol thought of	Symbol spun	Match?
1.	△	○	No
2.	○	□	No
3.	⬡	⬡	Yes

You will need a spinner and cards marked with the symbols shown. Spinning the spinner simulates how guessing would work.

Place the cards down faceup. One partner concentrates on a symbol and draws it secretly on the chart. The other partner spins the spinner and records the symbol on the chart. After 12 tries, the partners record the number of times both symbols match.

Answer the questions, based on your simulation.

1. How many times did the symbols match? ______________

2. Could a person expect to match some of the symbols by guessing? ______________

3. What is the probability of guessing a symbol correctly? ______________

4. How does this compare with your answer to Question 1? ______________

Name ______________________________

Investigating Perimeter

Work in teams of two. Each team should have scissors and a ball of string. You will cut lengths of string equal to the perimeter of:

- a student desktop
- a chalkboard
- the classroom door

Each team must measure the same items.

You may use your own techniques for finding perimeters. You may not, however, use materials other than the scissors and string.

When all teams finish, meet as a class. Discuss the techniques used for finding perimeter. Compare the lengths of string cut for each object.

Each team may then use a tape measure to measure the perimeters. Compare these measurements to the strings cut earlier. Now discuss how you think formulas were developed for finding perimeter and why you think tools such as tape measures are used for measuring.

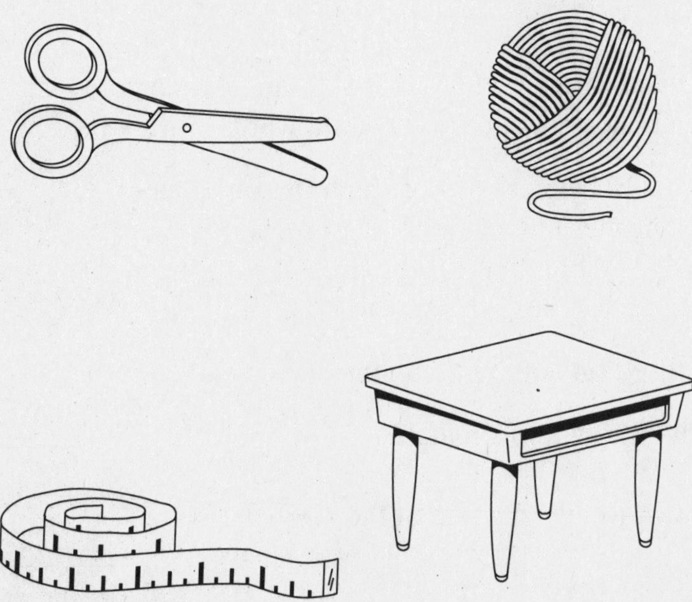

Name ______________________________

At the Movies

Attendance so far this season at the Movierama Drive-In is recorded below.

Week of Attendance	Week of Attendance	Week of Attendance	Week of Attendance
June 22: 1,562 29: 1,704 Total June: 3,266	July 6: 1,851 13: 1,072 20: 2,320 27: 2,759 Total July:	August 3: 1,752 10: 1,432 17: 2,061 24: 1,141 Total August:	September 1: 8: Total September:

Examine the attendance figures. Then answer the questions.

1. Estimate the total attendance for July. Then use a calculator to give the exact attendance. ________

2. Give an estimated and exact attendance figure for August. ________

3. Total attendance for September is usually 10% less than for June. Estimate September's total attendance. ________

4. Total attendance was 16,500 last year. Will Movierama do better this year? Explain your answer.

____

____

Name ______________________________

Lisa's Lunch Shop

Lisa wants to order new carpet for her restaurant. She does not need to cover the area beneath the salad bar and booths.

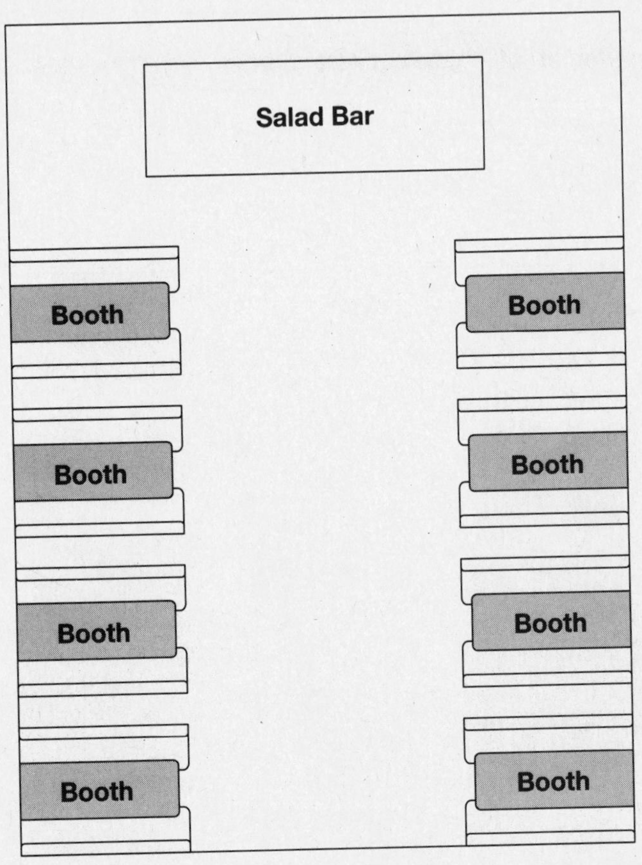

Examine the diagram. Then answer the questions, using a calculator if needed.

1. The length of the restaurant is 26 feet. The width is 20 feet. What is the total area? ______________

2. Each booth measures 5.5 feet long and 4 feet wide. Give the area covered by one booth. By all the booths. ______________

3. The salad bar is 11 feet long and 3.5 feet wide. How much of the floor does it cover? ______________

4. With a pencil, shade the portion of floor to be carpeted. Using what you know, find the area to be carpeted. ______________

Name ______________________________

Figure It Out

Figure A is a diagram of the playground at the new park.
Figure B is a diagram of a sandbox.

Figure A

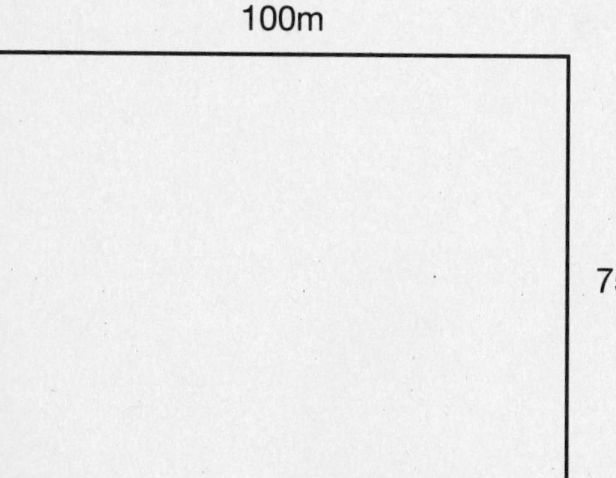

Area = 7,500 m^2

Figure B

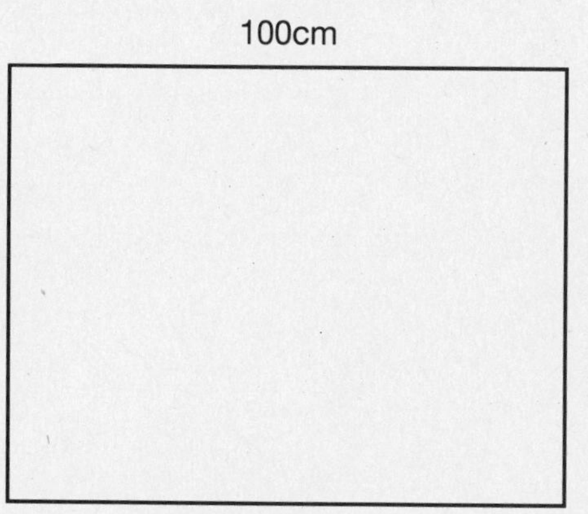

Area = 7,500 cm^2

Compare the two figures and their measurements.
Then answer the questions.

1. Write the area, **7,500 m^2** or **7,500 cm^2,** you think is closest to the area of the following:

a picture frame	____________	a gymnasium	____________
a doghouse roof	____________	a football field	____________
a wading pool	____________	a parking lot	____________
a soccer field	____________	a tablecloth	____________

2. List things in your classroom that might have an area of 7,500 square centimeters.

Compare your answers with your classmates. ______________________________

____

Name ________________________________

Making Sails

Gina's class is making sails for their model sailboats. All the sails are right triangles. Solve the problems, using what you know about the area of right triangles.

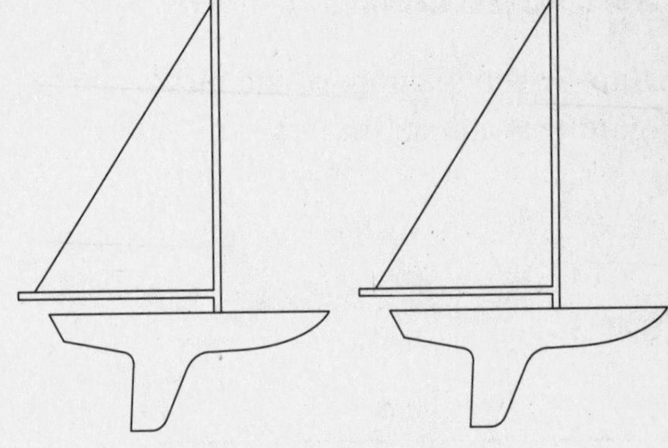

1. One of Gina's sails had a base of 22 cm and a height of 47 cm. Give its area. ____________

2. Gina made another sail with a base of 19 cm and a height of 48 cm. Is this sail larger? ____________

3. Paul made three sails that measured:
$b = 25$ cm, $h = 47$ cm
$b = 15$ cm, $h = 45$ cm
$b = 26$ cm, $h = 59$ cm
What is their total area? ____________

4. Sara measured her three sails:
$b = 21$ cm, $h = 34$ cm
$b = 19$ cm, $h = 47$ cm
$b = 18$ cm, $h = 51$ cm
Whose sails have a greater area, Paul's or Sara's? Verify your answer. ____________

Name ______________________________

Try It with Triangles

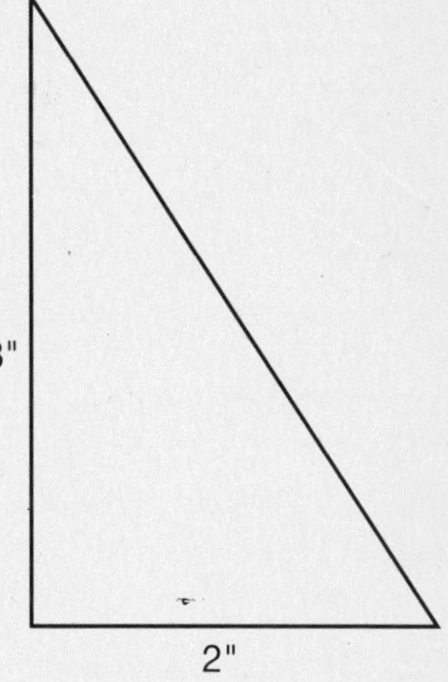

Trace this triangular figure and cut it out. Use it to complete the described drawings on a separate piece of paper. Compare your results with your classmates.

1. Trace the triangular figure and color it yellow. List five things you see or use every day that contain a triangular shape.

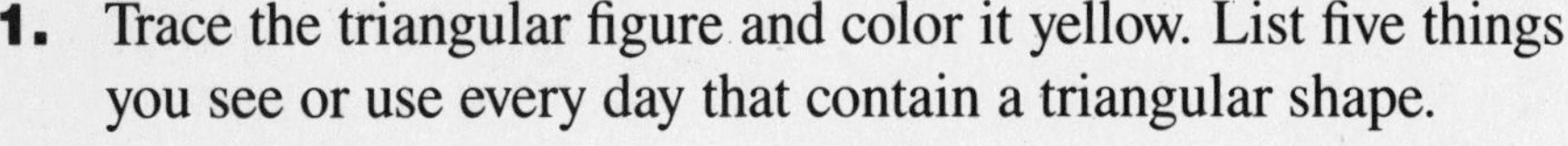

____

____

2. Use the figure to draw three different figures, each with an area of 6 square inches. Color them blue.

3. Draw two different figures, each with an area of 12 square inches. Color them red.

4. Visualize a triangle with $\frac{1}{2}$ the area of your triangular figure. Develop a method for drawing the smaller triangle, using your triangular figure. Color the smaller triangle black.

5. Make a repeating design, using your triangular figure. Color it any color you choose. Be able to tell the total area of your design.

Name ______________________________

Areas of Paralellograms

The base and height are given for each paralellogram. Estimate the area.

1. $b = 8.3$ mm, $h = 7.18$ mm $A =$ ____________

2. $b = 24.66$ cm, $h = 6.8$ cm $A =$ ____________

3. $b = 8.17$ m, $h = 3.99$ m $A =$ ____________

4. $b = 12.46$ cm, $h = 9.7$ cm $A =$ ____________

5. $b = 36.8$ mm, $h = 10.10$ mm $A =$ ____________

6. $b = 18.72$ mm, $h = 4.66$ mm $A =$ ____________

How much paper is needed to make each shape?

7.

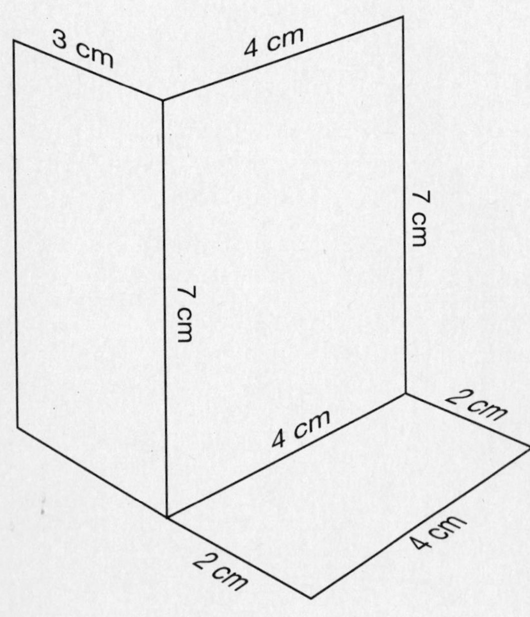

____

8.

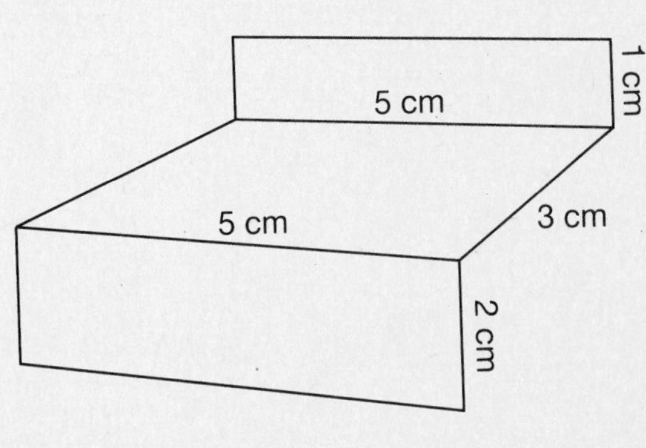

____

Name ___

Developing Consumer Skills

Dear Family,

Your child has been learning how to determine volume. Do this activity together, to help develop his or her consumer skills regarding major appliances.

Compute the volume of your refrigerator or freezer. Discuss how the volume relates to your family's needs. Contrast this with the needs of smaller and larger households. Consider the pros and cons of purchasing an appliance with more or less volume. Be sure to consider cost of electricity.

If possible, visit an appliance store. Estimate the volume of several models before comparing them to the sticker dimensions. Notice how volume is advertised and how it affects price.

Name ______________________________

Finding Surface Area

1. Jenny wants to cover storage boxes with contact paper. The dimensions of the first box are:

Front: $3' \times 2'$

Back: $3' \times 2'$

Top: $3' \times 1\frac{1}{2}'$

What is its surface area? ______________

2. Jenny has three other boxes to cover. The second box is the same size as the first, but the third measures:

Front: $3' \times 1\frac{1}{2}'$

Back: $3' \times 1\frac{1}{2}'$

Top: $3' \times 1'$

Give the total surface area for these three boxes. ______________

3. The last box is twice as large as the first two. What is its surface area? ______________

4. Give the total surface area Jenny needs to cover on the four boxes. ______________

5. Contact paper is \$0.29 a square foot. Use mental math to estimate the change Jenny will receive from \$50. ______________